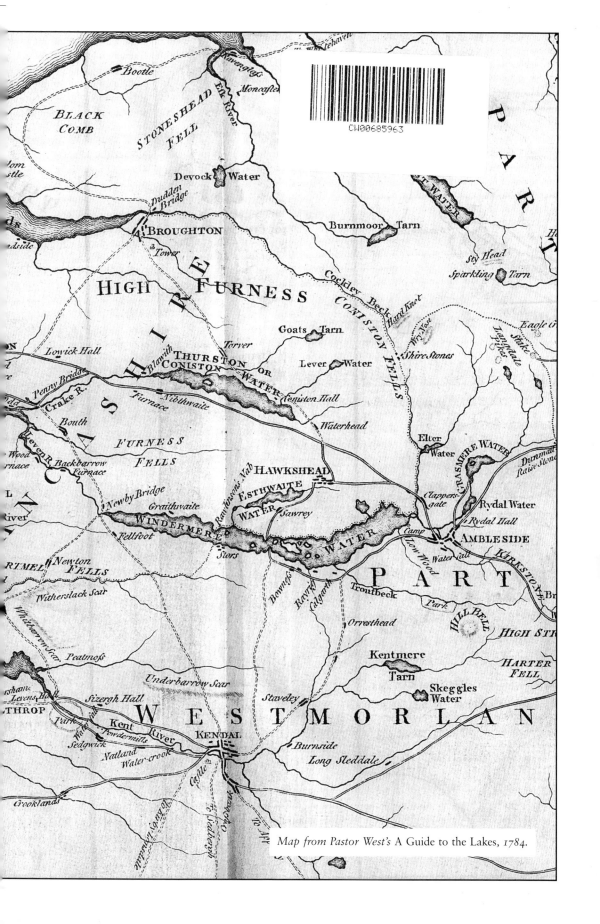

Map from Pastor West's A Guide to the Lakes, *1784.*

AROUND MORECAMBE BAY

A Flookburgh fisherman with horse-drawn cart.

AROUND MORECAMBE BAY

W.R. Mitchell

Phillimore

2005

Published by
PHILLIMORE & CO. LTD,
Shopwyke Manor Barn, Chichester, West Sussex, England

ISBN 1 86077 331 1

Printed and bound in Great Britain by
THE CROMWELL PRESS LTD
Trowbridge, Wiltshire

CONTENTS

To
Basil Rowbotham
who painted Cartmel Priory
by moonlight

LIST OF ILLUSTRATIONS

Frontispiece: Flookburgh Fisherman

ACKNOWLEDGEMENTS

When, in 1951, I began a spell of almost forty years as the editor of *Cumbria* magazine, three counties – Cumberland, Westmorland and Lancashire – had territorial claims on the Lake District, which, being sea-washed on three sides, gave my writings a maritime flavour. The 1950s was a good time to study Morecambe Bay, its environs and its people, many of whom were – until local government reorganisation in 1974 – dwelling in what was grandly known as Lancashire North of the Sands. Life was unhurried. Old crafts flourished. I chatted with fisherfolk who went on to the Bay at low tide with horses and carts. There were trade links between the Bay and the extensive coppice woods, where blue-grey smoke rose from charcoal pits.

My interest in local life was quickened when I read Tom Pape's book, *The Sands of Morecambe Bay*. Tom contributed handwritten articles to *Cumbria*. I got to know William Burrows and Alfred Butler, guides to the Kent and Levens Sands respectively. In 1951, when royalty visited Lancaster on the 600th anniversary of the creation of Lancashire as a County Palatine, these two men carried seven quarts of Morecambe Bay shrimp to the city. Cedric Robinson, successor as guide to the Kent Sands, became (and still is) a good friend. He was on hand when I made the first of many crossings of the oversands route, from Hest Bank to Kent's Bank, in the 1960s. We covered the eight miles at a sprightly pace and, it being a bright summer day, several of us walked the eight miles back to rejoin our cars.

In 1986 Cedric collaborated with me in compiling a picture book, *Life Around Morecambe Bay*, the foreword to which was contributed by the Duke of Edinburgh. Cedric had sat beside the Duke in 1975 when he headed a cavalcade of horse-drawn carriages across the sand before visiting Holker for the Horse Driving Trials of 1975. He wrote that, having seen Morecambe Bay from the air, he was now able to see the full beauty of the Sands in their setting of Lakeland hills, 'and to experience the very special atmosphere of that unique place'. The cover of our book featured two of Peter Cherry's stunning photographs of fishing activity. Cedric Robinson introduced me to his father, William Robinson of Flookburgh, who wore two traditional items of apparel for a local fisherman: a blue gansey (jersey) and flat cap. Visiting him just after he had celebrated his 100th birthday, I heard him say, 'I'm having a good day. Get your tape-recorder out.' At a neighbouring house, owned by a fisherman, I examined some of the tackle used on the Sands. When I left, the fisherman's wife handed me some potted shrimp. It was one of many delightful days that I spent with the bayside folk.

I first became a regular visitor to South Walney when it was designated a nature reserve. Walter Shepherd was my guide. The progress of the nesting season in a vast gullery might be gauged by the appearance of Walter Shepherd's trilby, which became white with bird-lime when the adult birds with young took defensive action as its owner followed one of the paths. Walter showed me my first eider duck on its nest, which it covered like a feathered tea cosy. He then led me to the western shore for a glimpse of the rare oyster-plant. I often visited John Wilson, long-time warden at Leighton Moss nature reserve, near Silverdale, where I spied bitterns and bearded tits in the extensive reed beds. Herbie and Tissie Fooks, of Hay Bridge, near Booth, introduced me to the wildlife, especially the Furness red deer, the finest free-ranging reds in the land.

The names of informants are mentioned in the text. Jack Allonby, of Spark Bridge, was my main source of information about woodland crafts, especially charcoal-burning and besom-making. Stott Park Bobbin Mill, now owned by English Heritage, was a joy to visit. The Field Studies Council at Castle Head, on what used to be Holme Island, long since tethered to the mainland by a causeway, gave me details of the life here of John 'Iron Mad' Wilkinson. I also received a list of artefacts and coins found when Holme Island was being landscaped in the 1780s – a list compiled by Dr Joseph Priestley, Wilkinson's brother-in-law.

Help has been given by the Morecambe Bay Partnership, which has an informative website. Susan Wilson, Local History Librarian of Lancaster, and Barbara Adams, of Ulverston Library, responded promptly to my inquiries. Arthur Lupton drew my attention to a story linking his celebrated uncle, Arthur Ransome, with the railway station at Greenodd. Christine Denmead of Ulverston drew the map.

Illustrations from the following sources are cordially acknowledged: Celia King, 3, 45, 92, 95; Lancaster Public Library, 5, 49, 50, 75, 138; Lancaster Museum, 53; E. Gower, 107; Richard Bancroft, 21, 132, 139, 140, 149; E. Jeffrey, 81, 86, 126; E. Jeffrey (drawn from author's photographs), 34, 38, 40, 61, 62, 88, 89, 109, 110, 136, 137, 143, 150. Photographs from the author's collection: 14, 55, 56, 57, 69, 70, 72, 76, 77, 78, 80, 99, 111, 113, 119. Uncredited photographs by the author.

An Overview

Morecambe Bay extends to the east of a line drawn from Fleetwood to Silecroft. Described as 'a great inner sea', our second largest bay is moody, challenging, treacherous and outstandingly beautiful, especially in clear weather, when it has a range of Lakeland fells as its backdrop. The bay might be shallow but the tidal range is impressively large, between 20 and 30 feet. A flow tide surges up the gutters, performs pincer movements around the sandbanks, bubbles and boils against inter-tidal scars known as *skears*, and spreads over thousands of acres of inter-tidal marsh. A bore that runs up Kent estuary, at up to nine knots, dissipates in a flurry of foam against the iron columns of a railway viaduct, which were sunk through 70 feet of sand to find a firm base.

At low tide Morecambe Bay resembles a tawny desert, 120 square miles of mudflats and sandflats. This is the largest continuous inter-tidal area in England. Turner and David Cox were two notable artists who portrayed walkers and horse-drawn coaches on the oversands route between Lancaster and Furness. Out in the bay, over several centuries, the folk heroes have been guides appointed by the Duchy of Lancaster. They marked a safe route by sticking branches known as *brobs* in the sand. Quicksands occurred where fickle rivers – Keer, Kent and Leven – shifted their channels and the sand had not yet compacted. Around the Bay lie over five per cent of the salt marshes of Britain, providing inter-tidal grazing for cattle and a wintering ground for yearling sheep from the fells.

Morecambe Bay is an area of superlatives. It has been designated a Special Site of Scientific Interest, and the Lake District National Park extends to the shore in the northern part of the Bay. The name Morecambe is said to mean 'sea bend'. Camden, a chronicler of Tudor days, wrote in *Britannia* in 1586 that 'this estuary is crooked and Moricambe signifies in British, a crooked sea'. Edwin Waugh, the Lancashire Victorian who was a dialect writer, humorist, and traveller to remote parts of the country knew it as 'the great crooked bay' and admired its 'picturesquely-irregular shores'. The name may have a Celtic connotation, *Myr-cym*, this being a term for the sea.

The title Morecambe Bay was first used towards the end of the 18th century for what had previously been prosaically known as 'Kent Sands'. Whitaker, in his *History of Manchester* (1771), believed that the 'Morecambe' mentioned by Ptolemy, the Greek philosopher, in his *Geographia* of around A.D. 150, related to this bay, even though the classical writer had specified north-west Britain. Thomas West (*c.*1720-79), possibly inspired by Whitaker, mentioned 'Morecambe Bay' in his book *The Antiquities of*

Furness (1774). Mapmakers took their lead from 18th-century antiquaries. So popular did the name Morecambe become that it was adopted when a small fishing village known as Poulton-le-Sands blossomed into a holiday resort.

Human settlement around Morecambe Bay dates from about 1700 to 1400 B.C. As the fell country was losing its Pleistocene chill, a scattering of people on Walney, one of a cluster of low-lying islands to the west of the Bay, lived austere lives here, dining on shellfish and anything else they could catch. Early mankind had the social instincts of their descendants, judging by their impressive assembly places, such as a double stone circle of gleaming limestone on Birkrigg Common, south of Ulverston, which is a splendid viewpoint for Morecambe Bay. Within the circle were cremated remains of the dead. Norse folk, arriving from Ireland and the Isle of Man, are recalled at Heysham by a hogsback tombstone dating from the period when Christianity was supplanting Norse mythology. The Norman scribes who compiled Domesday Book in 1086 found Furness to be so isolated that most of the land to the north was under the control of Scottish kingdoms and therefore beyond their remit. The area was one of the hundreds of Lancashire, extending northwards from Garstang. Two portions were recognised, Lonsdale North and South of the Sands.

Most people writing about human associations with Morecambe Bay are preoccupied by the hazards of the low tide route from Hest Bank to Kents Bank, which uses the Cartmel peninsula as a 'stepping stone' before crossing Leven sands to reach Furness. The lives of the inhabitants of farms and villages around the Bay are equally fascinating. Farmers, fishermen, miners and workers in the coppice woods all had a connection with the Bay, either directly or through their products. Before Morecambe Bay silted up, boats of all types sailed to and from innumerable little ports, jetties and creeks. The first tourists were enthralled by fisherfolk who, at low tide, and with horse-drawn carts, recovered a harvest of edible creatures, notably shrimps and cockles. Edwin Waugh could not be persuaded to 'walk the sands' but, instead, provided us with an insight into life around the margin. A prodigious writer with a large following, Waugh saw brown-faced fishermen at Silverdale station, with bags of cockles and hampers of fluke (flounders) that were to be despatched to the southern markets by the next train. At the *Crown* in Grange, Waugh listened as Aad Billy, the blind fiddler, 'who lives by scattering music among the folk of Cartmel Fells', played 'Scots wha hae wi' Wallace bled', beating time with his foot and uttering a curious croon. After visiting what remains of Gleaston Castle, near Great Urswick, Waugh 'hunted around for food'. He found it in a clean little hostelry, dining on eggs and bacon, cheese, ale, salad (fresh from the garden behind the house), and buttermilk, 'in addition to which I had my shoe mended'. The bill totalled 3s. 6d.

The wildlife on and around Morecambe Bay is exceptional. The Bay itself has been designated a European Marine Site, a Special Area of Conservation and a Wetland of International Importance. The area around the Bay abounds with birds and beasts. The Furness red deer take cover in deciduous woods and graze the mosses while roe deer flit, as insubstantial as shadows, through old coppice woods where once there was the reek of smoke from charcoal pitsteads. At Leighton Moss, in a huge reed bed with stretches of open water in a quiet valley on the eastern edge of the Bay, nest bitterns, marsh harriers and bearded tits. At dusk the flute-like whistle of the otter is heard beside unpolluted rivers. Salmon and sea trout, against the national trend, fare well on the Lune and Kent. A decline in fish stocks in the Leven might be accounted for by the sad state of Windermere, our largest lake, where recent changes are being keenly monitored.

Morecambe Bay supports 20,000 breeding seabirds and an estimated 244,000 birds from more northerly climes that sojourn here in winter. Knot and dunlin in their thousands perform tight aerial manoeuvres along the tideline, or, at high water, have favoured stretches of salt marsh where they sleep, heads under scapulars, waiting for the tide to turn and expose food in the form of tiny living creatures. The oystercatcher, a pied bird with a shrill voice, which primarily dines on cockles, is well represented here, its numbers peaking at well over 50,000. An estimated 12,000 curlew dip their long, curved bills in the mud for food and occasionally utter their fluty call – a true sound of the wilderness. Shelduck nest in profusion in old rabbit burrows, and lead their attractively striped young ahead of themselves in line, hoping to avoid the attention of hungry gulls, which, on Walney Island, form the largest mixed colony of herring and lesser black-backed gulls in Europe. Walney is also the southernmost nesting place for eiders.

The Morecambe Bay Partnership mentions other things that make Morecambe Bay special: unique views of the Lakeland Fells, the vast expanse of tidal sandflats, the tranquillity, the shifting sands, the light and, last but not least, the sense of history and heritage.

Change is inevitable. A recent conspicuous example was the appearance at Heysham of the blocky form of an atomic power station. Just over the horizon, beyond the entrance to Morecambe Bay, enormous rigs mark the spot where an estimated reserve of six trillion cubic feet of natural gas is being tapped. There is enough on hand to meet 10 per cent of the country's gas needs. The gas is pumped ashore at Barrow-in-Furness. The Crown Estate has also awarded a lease for offshore wind energy to be generated; some of the turbines will be situated off Walney Island.

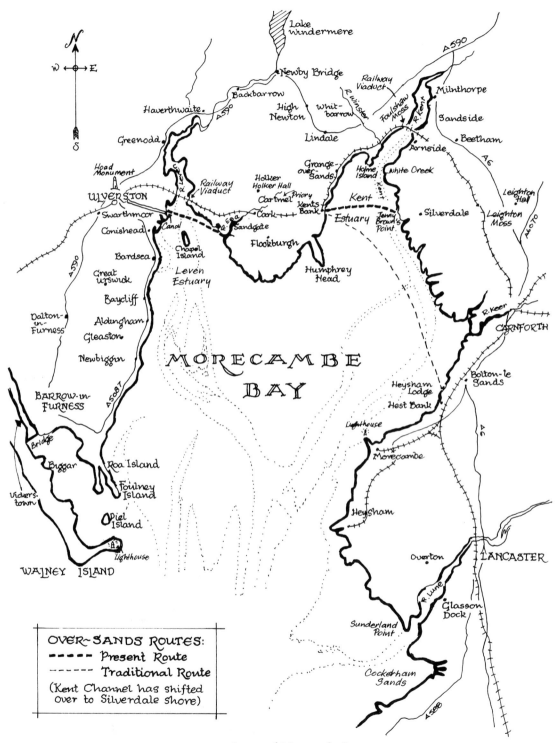

1   *A map of Morecambe Bay.*

One

THE BAY

Morecambe Bay, shallow and saucer-shaped, has a bedrock composed of limestone, formed from the skeletal remains of animals that lived in a warm sea some 340 million years ago, when what is now Britain was part of a land mass slowly drifting northwards from the equator. The Bay holds sediment from the glacial ice that sculpted the Lakeland valleys. Glacial mush, known as boulder clay, formed drumlins, small, rounded hills that are especially noticeable in the northern part. Alien rocks include greenstone washed down from Lakeland and red granite from Shap. Prominent scars give highspots to the northern shore between Aldingham and Bardsea. Elsewhere the pearl-white limestone is offset by the New Red Sandstone of Furness and the Red Marl of Morecambe and Heysham. The blue-grey Silurian Slates of South Lakeland extend to the estuary of the Leven.

Limestone, the use of which gives villages and farms a cheerful aspect, is especially attractive where it has been smoothed by glacial action into 'pavements', consisting of blocks known as 'clints' with crevices in between termed 'grykes'. Whitbarrow (flat-topped 'white hill'), at 700 feet, and Yewbarrow Crag are prominent examples. The view in fine weather from a hospice erected on Hampsfell above Grange in 1834 takes in Snowdon and the Isle of Man. The Bay is a young land- and seascape, forever changing at the whim of weather, river and tide. The Nature Conservancy, conducting research into the Bay as part of a barrage feasibility study, found it had been progressively silting since the 11th century, the process being augmented by artificial reclamation in the upper estuaries.

2   *The Sands of Morecambe Bay.*

3 *A coach crossing the Kent estuary.*

What the sea gave it was inclined to take away again. In a noteworthy inundation in the middle of the 16th century whole villages were swept away. In 1677 marshland at Bolton-le-Sands was eroded and, about the same time, new land appeared at Winder Moor, on the Cartmel coast. Saltwater used to flow round a mound on which the housing estate of Ravenstown now stands. A natural silting-up process was accelerated when, in the 1850s, the Furness Railway Company set bands of iron around the Bay. Where viaducts were built across estuaries, new land, sand and gravel were reclaimed – to be fought over in the courts by the railway company and aggrieved landowners. With the coming of the railway, the village of Grange acquired an artificial shoreline and a combined sea wall and promenade, causing it to burgeon as a holiday resort. Some still recall the pier that was once at Grange. Coastal vessels formerly frequented the cove at Silverdale, which is now barely covered by the tide. A spectacular storm in 1977 inflicted extensive damage on the coastline and, overnight, led to the mighty Kent switching from the Grange side of the bay to that at Silverdale. The storm demolished the South Pier at Morecambe, which was not replaced. Another storm, in 1982, badly damaged the stone pier at Arnside.

For a millennium the Sands separated the main part of the Red Rose County from its northern territory, which became known as Lancashire North of the Sands. The name Furness – 'far ness' – testified to its isolation. W.G. Collingwood, the Lakeland historian, wrote of Lancaster as being the natural county town for the northern shore of Morecambe Bay. How much more was this so, he queried, when the Cumbrian Hills were impassable with forest and swamp, "wild beasts and wild folk"? Collingwood added that the blue of a coloured map might cut Lancashire into two, 'but the sands really join Furness and Cartmel with the opposite coast, making it an easy natural road'. In 1974 the Boundary Commissioners linked Lancashire North of the Sands with Cumberland and Westmorland to form a single local government entity named Cumbria.

Did the Romans use the oversands route to avoid ambush by natives? Furness was not garrisoned but, judging by chance finds of coins at Ulverston and Grange-over-Sands, locals were aware of the Romans. In 1800 a hoard of 600 coins, the most recent minted in A.D. 250, was found in a pot in Park Wood, Cartmel. Before turnpike roads and the Furness Railway made overland journeys round the Bay tolerable, travellers crossed 'those dreary, wet sands'. At low tide a motley group, composed of people on foot or horseback or passengers in horse-drawn coaches, travelled on a route that was never precisely defined, for each tide swept away the prints of foot and wheel. The route effected a majestic curve, beginning at Hest Bank and ending at Kents Bank, crossing the estuaries of two rivers. At a point near Silverdale travellers would have been half a mile from the shore.

Going over the Sands was quicker and easier for travellers from Lancaster to Furness than trekking over land. A milestone at Cartmel gave the distance to Lancaster 'over sands' as 15 miles, less than half that of the rough old route via Kendal. From Cartmel to Ulverston 'over sands' was a mere seven miles, as opposed to 11 miles by land. Crossing Kent Sands was indeed part of a daring west coast route between Lancaster and Whitehaven. Long-distance travellers forded the rivers Keer, Kent, Leven, Duddon and the shallow area where the Esk, Mite and Irt pour their clear, cool water into the sea near Ravenglass. Medieval travellers on the oversands route did not have the benefit of compass or printed tide-table. Some would be inclined to set off from shore at the wrong state of the tide or would lose their sense of direction in mist; strong currents in the rivers Kent and Leven could be death-traps to the unwary.

The sands of Morecambe Bay have a magnificent backdrop in the Lakeland fells. From the seafront at Fleetwood (a once-busy fishing port) a clear-weather view takes in a range of blue-grey hills extending from Black Combe to Ingleborough. Celia Fiennes, journeying through England in 1698, gazed at the Bay from the tower of Lancaster Castle but did not experience the sands route. Celia saw the town, the river and 'the sea beyond … and the great hills there called Furness Fells'. Aesthetic types loved a spell in the wilderness of the bay at low tide before reaching the 'promised land' of the Lake District. To the Romantics of the late 18th and early 19th centuries, the prospect was exhilarating. William Wordsworth wrote that this oversands route was to be regarded not just as a deed of derring-do but also as 'a decided proof of taste'.

4   *Lancaster Sands.*

The artist Turner, who crossed the sands on his northern tours of 1816 and 1825, made hurried sketches that he would later work up into dramatic paintings. He depicted the Lancaster coach emerging from the Bay, dripping from a heavy shower, and in another picture showed passengers newly arrived at Hest Bank on a sunlit day. A Cumbrian poet, Norman Nicholson, walking on the sands near his native town of Millom, considered that, to 18th-century travellers, crossing the Bay would be 'a tremendous curtain-raiser to their tour of the Lakes'. He was also aware that material washed down from the Lakeland heights lay in the Bay, observing: 'Look at Morecambe Bay when the tide is out and you are looking at the mountains and hills brought low.'

A few years after the trauma of a raid by Scots led by Robert Bruce in 1322, the King and his Council looked favourably on a request by the Abbot of Furness for the appointment of a local coroner. The nearest coroner was at Lancaster. A confirmatory grant declared that:

> by reason of the violence and strength of the current at the ebb and flow of the tide, many people in crossing the sands between Furness and adjacent parts had before that time been exposed to peril, upon whose bodies the office of Coroner had not been hitherto duly executed, because the Coroners dwelt in distant parts.

The Prior of Cartmel appointed a guide for the Kent Sands. The Leven guide was an appointee of Conishead Priory. These men, having daily acquaintance with the Bay, were charged with preventing, as far as possible, the occurrence of accidents to travellers across low-tide Morecambe Bay.

The first mention of a guide was in 1501, when a man simply referred to as Edmondson held 'Carter House' and 10 acres of land in Cartmel, as well as the office of 'Carter upon the Sands' as tenant right from the Prior of Cartmel. In 1533 – when the Dissolution of the Monasteries was a burning topic – a young scholar

5 *Crossing Lancaster Sands, an old drawing based on a Turner painting.*

named John Leland and his friend John
Bale were permitted by Henry VIII to
search monastic libraries for works by
ancient writers. It was a task spread
over six years. Leland referred to but
avoided the oversands route, recording
that 'if I had kept the hy shore way
from Lancastre to Cumbreland I should
have gone by Cartemaile sand, wher a
fresch water doth cum ... to Conyhed
sande, whither a river resortith ... to
Duddon sands.' Within a short time the
appointment of guides, with their daily
knowledge of the topography of the
Bay – of its banks, sands and wharfs
– had become established. Between
1564 and 1836 no fewer than 14 of
Edmondson's successors as guides to
the Kent Sands came from the Carter
family.

An unbroken succession of guides
spans the 470 years between the Dissolution of the Monasteries and the
present day. Such guides have been
maintained out of the revenues of the
Duchy of Lancaster, the appointment
and management of a guide being dealt

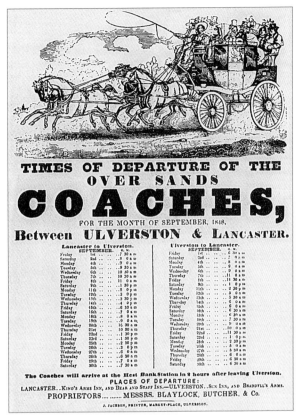

6   *Oversands coaches.*

with by three local trustees. The Carters of old received a formal sum called Peter's
pence and the use of a house and tract of land in Cart Lane, Kents Bank. They came
into their own when the tide had ebbed for about four hours, riding white horses and
stopping periodically to prod the channel with a long pole and then to plant *brobs*
(made of birch or broom) in the sand to mark the best fording place on the Kent. The
brobs were set at a considerable depth to avoid the clutches of the tides. The guide
indicated his position by blowing a horn, and when the incoming tide was imminent
he blew the horn as a warning before hastening back to the shore.

In monastic times the crossing parties would have included travellers as fascinating
and diverse as Chaucer's pilgrims. The Abbot of Furness and his retinue crossed on
their way to Lancaster; other Furness monks attended a fishery at Halton on the
Lune. One of the rock outcrops became known as Priest Skeer. At such places the
imagination was fired by tales of conger eels which could reach six feet in length and
60 pounds in weight. With the tide just over the low horizon, a traveller needed little
encouragement to walk briskly. Special care was taken at the estuaries, especially those
of Keer and Kent which, according to an old couplet, 'have parted many a good man
and his meeare [mare]'. In summer, when low tides and lack of rain permitted the
high sands to dry out, deposits of salt would make the Bay gleam.

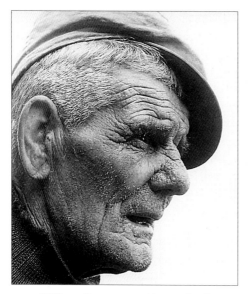

7 *William Burrows, guide to the Kent Sands.*

With Cartmel peninsula assuming the role of a stepping-stone on the west coast route, guide posts were essential. The Headless Cross at the intersection of roads probably signified to northbound travellers the completion of a safe crossing of Kent Sands, while those travelling in the opposite direction might stop to utter a prayer for a safe crossing. The registers of Cartmel Priory up to 1880 record the deaths of 141 people overtaken by the tide or enveloped in quicksands. The toll would be higher when other records were taken into account. Overall, there would be one or two fatalities a year, a trifling figure in view of the numbers using the route.

An early entry, in September 1576, relates to a young man 'which was drowned in the broad waters'. In August 1577 there was recovered from the Bay 'one little man round faced which was drowned at Grainge'. On the floor of the south-west area of the Priory Church of Cartmel is a gravestone of 1780 with two inscriptions and some verses. Commemorated here are Robert Harrison who, aged 24 years, was drowned 'on Lancaster Sands', and his mother, Margaret, who drowned at almost the same place three years later. Possibly she died while making a pilgrimage to the spot where her son lost his life. The accompanying verse would send a chill down the spine of those who read it:

> The waves they do compass me
> And no assistance can I see
> Which makes me to lament and cry
> Lord send me help least here I die.
> It is in vain for to withstand
> What is decreed by God's command.
> My dying day I cannot shun
> Farewell dear friends
> My glass is run.

In mist it was easy for a traveller to become disorientated. At an inquest on Frederick Postlethwaite, in 1835, two separate depositions were taken. James Bell testified that he found the body 'up Lancaster sands, in the direction of Know Hill ... I verily believe that he came to his death in attempting to cross the sands'. The second deponent, Thomas Smith, had seen Postlethwaite depart on horseback and accompanied him in a *shandry* cart part of the way. He had no doubt that the deceased 'got confused by the mist on the sands and lost himself when the tide came and drowned him'.

John Wilkinson, ironmaster, who had an estate at Castle Head, near Lindale, was buried four times – after his death at his Midlands home, then as his iron coffin was being borne across Kent Sands to his beloved Castle Head, a threatening tide led to it being left far from land. When it was recovered on the ebb it had been buried in sand. Interred at Castle Head, it was removed to a pauper's grave at Lindale.

A testy John Wesley, who traversed the whole route (Kent, Leven, Duddon and Esk) in 1759 as he headed for Whitehaven, confided in his Journal that the sands were so far from each other 'it is scarce possible to pass them all in one day'. This would not appeal to Wesley, a man in a hurry who, all along the way, had encountered

> a generation of liars, who detain all strangers as long as they can, either for their own gain or their neighbours. I can advise no stranger to go this way. He may go round by Kendal and Keswick, often in less time, always with less expense and far less trial of his patience.

Pennant, on a horseback 'Tour' of 1769, undertook

> a melancholy ride of 11 miles; the prospect on all sides quite savage; high barren hills indented by the sea or dreary wet sands rendered more horrible by the approach of night and a tempestuous evening. Before us was an extensive but shallow ford, formed by the Kent, now crossed with trouble by the beating of the waves. At the entrance into the water we are met by a guide called here 'the carter', who is maintained by the public and is obliged in all weathers to attend here, from sunrise to sunset, in order to conduct passengers over the sands.

In 1792 Adam Walker crossed both the Kent and Leven Sands:

> We cross also two rivers, each sometimes more than half a mile wide. This sounds alarming! But it is seldom that they are more than a foot deep. Indeed, I have crossed them when we were obliged to open the two doors of the chaise and let the water run through; but this is seldom the case. Fatal accidents happen. Sometimes they are ludicrous. A Gentleman's horse was some time ago drowned in crossing one of these rivers too late. The horse floated, and the Gentleman stuck to him, as a wrecked seaman would to a plank. The Man and Horse were carried up by the tide a considerable way inland and so near that shore that he tried by the long tail of the Horse if he could touch the bottom. No bottom was to be found! The tide turned, and the Man and Horse began to move towards the main sea! His heart sunk within him, though he still swam by the assistance of the Horse's tail. Several miles was he carried by this uncouth navigation, when once more he was determined to try if he was within soundings. Having fastened one hand in the Horse's tail, he plunged into the sea, and think what must have been his feelings when he felt the bottom! Providence had placed him on a sand-bank! He stood up to the chin – the waves went over him – he disengaged himself from his good friend the dead Horse, and waited there till the tide forsook the Sands, and got safe home.

Ann Ratcliffe, another 18th-century traveller, crossed the 'trackless wastes' of the Leven estuary from Ulverston behind the early morning tide. The guide was going to his station on a sandbar near the first ford, 'where he remains to conduct passengers across the united streams of Crake and Leven till the returning tide washes him off'. Ann and her companions heard 'the shrill small cry of sea gulls, unseen, near an island that began to dawn through the mist'. As the mist lifted, she saw 'fishermen with carts and nets stealing along the margin of the tide'. Little boats were putting off from the shore. The 'wide desolation of the sands was animated only by some horsemen riding remotely in

8   *Alfred Butler, who guided travellers across the Leven estuary.*

groups towards Lancaster – and a mussel fisher in his cart trying to ford the channel we were approaching'. Shellfish gathered on the Furness side were eventually transported to Hest Bank by horse and cart and transferred to canal boats for delivery to the Lancashire towns.

Carriers would, for a fee, convey goods on the oversands route. John Higgins, a 17th-century carrier, arrived at Swarthmoor Hall with 'letters, iron ore, hopps, red herrings, books, sugar, vinegar, meat paper, oysters, phisical [*sic*] things and chocolatta'. Luke Barker, a contemporary of Higgins, conveyed 'over Sands' the household goods of Margaret and Charles Taylor.

While crossing the Leven Sands from Holkergate to Ulverston, Wordsworth heard from a passing horseman the news that Robespierre had died. The poet 'stood on this perilous waste of sands to shout aloud anthems of thanksgiving for this great vindication of eternal justice'. He jotted down his memories of the occasion, having seen

> A variegated crowd
> Of vehicles and travellers, horse and foot,
> Wading beneath the conduct of their guide
> In loose procession through the shallow stream
> Of inland waters.

In 1781 a daily coach service across the sands between Lancaster and Ulverston became instantly popular, being a handy alternative to a long, bone-shaking detour by road. The *Cumberland Pacquet* ran three times a week between the *Sun Inn* at Lancaster and the *King's Arms* at Ulverston at a charge of 5s. a passenger. Setting off one day, the coach returned on the next 'as the tide will permit'. The travelling public was assured that the driver was sober, careful and well acquainted with the sands. It was humbly hoped that the owner's plan would meet with due encouragement, 'as this is the most cheap, safe and expeditious method of crossing the sands to and from Ulverston'. The northbound coach crossed the river bridge and at Slyne, some three miles up the road, left it for Hest Bank, where carts and other vehicles awaited the Sands Guide. A lantern, kindled at dusk in a top room at the *Hest Bank Hotel*, acted as a guide to those who had not yet reached the shore.

During a crossing of Kent Sands horses might plunge up to their bellies at the rivers. In extreme circumstances coach passengers retracted their legs. When fractious horses came to a halt on a soft river bed the narrow wheels of the coach would sink, creating alarm. A coach that crossed in 1811 developed a list and the 15 passengers were tipped into the channel; the horses were detached and everyone travelled safely to land – on horseback. The coach vanished from sight and the luggage carried on top was swept away by the next tide. When another coach was blown over by an especially lively wind it was righted and continued to operate for another seven years before being lost in quicksands.

William Green, in *The Tourist's New Guide* (1819), penned an introduction to the Bay that was guaranteed to scare timid readers: 'As he [the traveller] pursues his often-trackless way, he will recollect that, probably but a few hours before, the whole expanse was covered with some fathoms of water and that in a few more it will as certainly be covered again.' In 1825 John Briggs, uneasy on reaching one of the Bay's mighty channels, said to his sister, 'We must either go back or swim over.' When they were driven into the water Briggs felt afraid for a moment, but 'my sister's vivacity soon dissipated my fears'. Those who could afford to be conveyed in style and with a minimum of danger used a 'diligence', a moderately light vehicle that carried a few people and was less likely than a coach to sink in soft sand. The *Lonsdale Magazine* of 1820 ran an article that began when the writer was aroused from sleep in a hotel in Lancaster. The coach driver burst into the room, shouting 'For God's sake make haste ... the tide is down ... if you delay, we shall all be drowned.'

Mrs Gaskell, Victorian novelist and biographer of Charlotte Brontë, who stayed at Gibraltar Farm, near Silverdale, described the Sands Guide as 'a square man sitting stern on his white horse, the better to be seen when daylight ebbs'. On foggy nights he blew a ram's horn trumpet 'to guide by the sound'. Miss A. Taylor's observations of life on the Bay in the 1830s are of special interest because they were edited by Miss A.M. Wakefield and published at Grange as *Cartmel Priory and Sketches of North Lonsdale*. Miss Wakefield dedicated her 'little book' to 'Her Highness Princess Marie Louise of Schleswig-Holstein, an admirer of the north-country'. At Hest Bank, Miss Taylor recalled, the large coach began to sway. 'Sometimes the horses plunged into the channel ... but after much whipping and splashing we were safe out of the water and landed on the sand again.' The guide, who arrived to 'pioneer the coachman over the dangerous cuts and quicksands', was strange and wild-looking, his long, unkempt hair appearing as rough as the sheepskin thrown across his old white horse. Having conducted the coach over the dangerous parts, he appeared at the carriage window and 'thrust in an old

9 *Cedric Robinson, the present Sands Guide, combines this work with fishing.*

cap, also made of sheepskin', asking for a recognition of his services; he then rode off once more to meet and conduct other travellers. When the sands had been impassable for weeks because of severe frosts, the guide might lead a long line of travellers, some on horseback, some on foot and as many as thirty or forty carriers' carts, 'looking like a caravan crossing the desert'.

The opening of a turnpike via Levens Bridge in 1820 did not greatly affect traffic on the Bay. The sands route was still much shorter and no tolls were involved. It was the opening of the Furness Railway in 1857 that sounded the death knell. Ironically, in that same year seven farm servants trudging to Lancaster to attend a hiring fair were overwhelmed by the tide. Their bodies were found the next day. With the coming of a reliable rail link round the Bay the Sands Guide was able to combine his work with more serious fishing. For the two centuries of the great droving days, when livestock was imported from Scotland and Ireland and driven on foot, some cattle bound for the English marts were driven across Kent Sands. Edwin Waugh, in a description of Silverdale in 1861, saw what must have been one of the last herds. He wrote, 'Now from the northward a great herd of cattle moves slowly over the solemn waste on their way from Kent's Bank to the Wharton shore.'

On 13 July 1907 Professor Stearne, of Manchester, swam from Morecambe to Grange-over-Sands in three hours 45 minutes 41 seconds. His feat initiated an annual race. The distance was judged to be between nine and 11 miles, depending on the state of the channels and the tide. Gerald Forsberg, in his book *Long Distance Swimming*, wrote:

10   *A guided walk from Silverdale to Kents Bank fords the Kent channel.*

> During the swimming season, the average sea water temperature is about two degrees lower than the Channel … Much fresh water also flows in from the Lakes, especially after heavy rainfall in the Lake District. At high tide, such cold fresh water is temporarily held in check but, as the ebb progresses, so increases the agonising painful cold-water patching. The swift-running ebb also kicks up a horridly rough little sea when the wind blows against it … It is long, cold, rough – challenging.

At the end of the Second World War, the nine-mile walk from Hest Bank to the Cartmel peninsula became a popular excursion for rambling clubs in the area. T. Pape recorded that on 14 June 1947 over 200 members of the Morecambe and district youth organisations received a civil

11   *The Duke of Edinburgh holds the reins during a carriage crossing in 1985.*

12   *The home of the Sands Guide in Cart Lane, Kents Bank.*

13   *An attractive sign for Cart Lane at Kent's Bank.*

welcome as they stepped ashore at Cart Lane. Also enjoyed – thanks to Morecambe and Heysham Rotarians – were tickets for a free tea at either the *Grand* or *Crown* hotels and railway tickets for the return journey from Grange to Hest Bank. Now people began to cross the Bay for pleasure. The year 1963 saw the retirement as guide to Kent Sands of William Burrows. Aged 75, he had held the post for 14 years and been a fisherman all his life. As guide, he was proud of the way he marked the route across Kent estuary with *brods*. They had to be sunk to a depth of at least three feet, so he prepared places for them using an iron bar five feet long. Two sons, Dick and Granville, and his nephew Jack 'followed the sands'; they also netted for fluke and took salmon from the Lune with the *haaf-net*. From his home at Canal Foot, Alfred Butler combined being a Sands Guide with fishing. In 1954 he told the author that during the first six months of the year there had been 53 crossings. He had also been in attendance when six horse-drawn carts and two saddle horses crossed the Leven Sands.

A change in the course of the Kent meant that Silverdale was now the starting point for the oversands route. The most publicised crossing occurred in 1985 when the Duke of Edinburgh, a devotee of carriage driving, crossed from Silverdale to Kents Bank with the present long-serving Sands Guide, Cedric Robinson, sitting beside him. The Duke led a cavalcade of horse-drawn carriages on a smooth, fast journey that was less exciting than a newspaper led its readers to believe when they wrote about a 'daring and historic bid' across 'the treacherous Morecambe Bay Sands'. The *brobs* used to mark the route were made from laurels on the Kents Bank side and rhododendrons near to Silverdale. At the deepest point of the Kent channel, the coaches were hardly axle deep, and the horses could maintain a smart, regular pace. At the crossing of the railway at Kents Bank, flagmen were in position and boards were laid down. Cedric Robinson, who has guided many thousands of people across Kent Sands, was also a tractor-and-trailer fisherman. He used a specially adapted tractor hauling a trailer and attained a speed of 20 miles per hour. When a north-westerly blew, he and his fellow fishermen would be chilled to the bone, while the residents of Grange were sheltered in the lee of the hills.

Two

Fishing Communities

Morecambe

At the beginning of the 19th century, when the first tourists arrived at what is now Morecambe, the tide had its back broken against a huge bank of shingle extending from the stone jetty to the Battery, a feature so called because the militia had mounted guns here. Northwards to Hest Bank, and also south of Heysham, towards Middleton, lay a salt marsh, frequented by wild geese. Blown sand had created a grassed-over hill called Foxholes. When a building boom took hold at Morecambe the owner, a Mr Lodge, disposed of the hill by selling it as sand. Thousands of cartloads were transported to building sites in the east of the burgeoning town. There was a reminder of the old days in a rhyme composed by Richard James (1592-1638), which was included in his *Iter Lancastrense*:

> Here through ye wasshie sholes
> We spye an owld man wading for ye soles
> And flukes and rayes, which ye last morning tide
> Had stayed in nets, or did att anchor ride
> Upon his hooks ... making, mending nett,
> Preparing hooks and baits, wherewith to gett
> Cod, whiting, place, uppon ye sandie shelvs,
> Where with to feede ye markett and ourselves.

At Morecambe, virtually all the fisherfolk lived in an area bounded by Marine Road, Lord Street, Poulton Road and Clarence Street. Among the well-known families were Benson and Butler, Shaw and Woodhouse. A distinctive form of speech used locally contained examples from Old Norse. Nicknames were also widely used: one man was called 'Tarr-o', a name relating to nets; 'Ganza' alluded to the gansey or jersey; 'Shir' may have come from an old custom of sharing the catch. Other unofficial names for fishermen were 'Shigger', 'Clyde', 'Lion' and 'Gaffer'. (The latter was the brother of 'Shir'.) A gathering place for gossip and the mending of nets was the Victorian shelter near the Green Street slipway. Anyone heading that way was said to be 'going to the top'. It was also handy for the premises of the fish merchants.

Most of the Morecambe men used nobbies, trawlers that when idle lay in an offshoot of the Grange Channel and were exposed to westerly gales. A trawlerman had to be back at the moorings three hours before low water or two hours after. One Christmas, in the 1870s, a gale sank 60 boats at their moorings. To relieve the resulting need among many fisherfolk Canon Gordon, a popular incumbent (and friend of the composer Edward Elgar, who helped with his music festival), met some of the men and formed the Morecambe Fishing Boat Insurance Company. Payment was made at the rate of 90 per cent of the total damage and the full amount in cases of total loss. Most Morecambe trawlers were built in the sheds of Crossfield Brothers' boatyard at Arnside, although a few came from the yards of Ted Woodhouse and Jim Gardner at Overton by the Lune. Crossfields also made rowing boats, and here was fashioned the dinghy called *Swallow* owned by the writer Arthur Ransome, who featured it in his classic children's tale *Swallows and Amazons*. In 1914 a rowing boat made of larch on an oak frame and varnished cost £3 10s.

A nobby had a mainsail and topsail. A foresail had been used on early models. Sail making was a cottage industry, which used a heavy cloth similar to linen purchased from one of the mills in Lancaster. Each piece was sewn on a domestic treadle machine during the winter months. Boats themselves were daubed with paint or tar. The proud owner of a new boat he was collecting was told: 'Ay, lad, it's great. If you tak it home and tar it, yon boat will last forivver.' The ballast used for nobbies was pig-iron.

Dick Woodhouse of Morecambe, who died in 1979, had a wide experience of trawlers in the 1920s, when sails were giving way to engines (in his case the Perkins diesel engine) and when, unknown to fishermen, local fishing was beginning a slow decline. Dick's daughter, Barbara, has special memories of two craft, *Mascot* and *Kelpie*. The former, which had a length of rather more than 30 feet, split open on a hard bank after being battered by a storm at her moorings near the Central Pier. *Kelpie*, named after a sea sprite, was 34 feet in length and had a distinctive colour scheme. Dick Woodhouse painted her lilac with a maroon trim; her decking was blue. He was proud of her registration – LR 1.

Sailing a trawler was a fine art, and it could not be rowed against the tide. Fishermen took great pride in their boats and their sailing skills, racing each other to the fishing grounds. They also competed in regattas and some of them manned the lifeboat, named after Sir William Priestley. Sebastian Ferranti, M.P., enjoyed a day's sailing in a Morecambe trawler. Morecambe fishermen were also well regarded by the wealthy members of the Royal Windermere Yacht Club, who hired some of them for races in the summer. Sir William Forewood, chairman of Cunard, hired Dick Woodhouse for the season. Woodhouse served Forewood well, but then fell out with him because he felt Forewood had been niggardly with money. When Dick ceased to work for Sir William, the latter's daughters – Faith, Hope and Charity – arrived at Dick's terraced house in Morecambe and pleaded with him to change his mind. They were unsuccessful.

Bill Baxter, of Morecambe, had many tales to tell of wild weather. His own father, Dick, was drowned when a sudden gale drove his trawler ashore near Blackpool. Once, when Bill was out with his brother, heavy seas and a biting wind grounded the trawler at the mouth of the Lune. The men managed to wade ashore. By the time they returned with help to reclaim the boat, it was obscured by sand and only the mast was in view. On one occasion a Morecambe trawlerman making for home in gusty weather, before the mudbanks had been covered by the tide, got lost when the sea became rough. In fog, he felt his way round the sandbanks haltingly, like a

14   *The stone jetty at Morecambe. The local trawler has the lines of a yacht.*

pedestrian making use of the pavement edge, listening all the while for the clang of hammers at a ship-breaking yard or even the clip-clop of horse-drawn vehicles on the Morecambe seafront. Although the fisherman carried a compass he did not consult it as frequently as a deep water fisherman would have done.

Walter Bell, a veteran fisherman, claimed that all the interest went out of fishing when boats were fitted with engines. He said that trawlermen were 't'same as farmers. We took a great interest in the weather. We didn't like a mackerel sky. "Mackerel sky – not twenty hours dry".' From the end of May until July, when there was a profusion of herring, the fishing took place well away from home. Morecambe men sailed northwards to Maryport and Whitehaven and southwards as far as Southport. In the best years, surplus herring were spread on the land as fertiliser. Plaice and sole were among the other fish caught; fluke, too, were relatively common. A Morecambe housewife would fry several fluke or poach them in milk. A special delicacy was skate wings.

Fishermen who had been staunchly independent eventually banded together, as Morecambe Trawlers Ltd, to market fish and shrimps. Professor C.E.M. Joad, a celebrated contributor to the *Brains Trust* on radio, was to call it 'perfect socialism at work'. The company offered tackle and waterproof clothing at competitive prices. A long shed was used for dipping nets in preservatives. Each member received a weekly payment and the annual profit was shared out on a percentage basis, relative

15 *The graceful lines of a Morecambe trawler. Few craft of this type remain. The pier has been demolished.*

to individual catches. It was closed down in the 1970s. Another co-operative effort was Morecambe Fishermen's Choir, members of which wore their dark trousers and ganseys almost as a uniform. The choir sang at the Fishermen's Chapel (Central Methodist, in Clarence Street) or in the open air. As God-fearing men, the choristers would not dream of working on a Sunday, nor even of going on a bus on that day. When they were booked to sing at Carnforth one Sunday they made the journey by foot. Half a century ago, with smaller families and wider opportunities, the number of fishermen was shrinking. When the cost of a new boat reached £1,000 there were gasps from the local men who could recall when a young man had a boat *given* to him by his father.

   Thora Hird, widely known as an actress in film and television productions, had vivid memories of her childhood at Morecambe. She told the author that the resort provided her with her first home and with a magical childhood. Her father, Jimmy, was a Todmorden man who, moving to Morecambe, became the manager of the Royalty theatre. The resort was then in the full flush of Edwardian vitality. Jimmy married a Miss Mayor and they lived in a house that 'went with the job' and was adjacent to the theatre. Thora, the second daughter, grew up in an affectionate family. She made her stage debut at the age of six weeks. Her mother carried her on to the stage of the Royalty in a play about a woman who had been 'done wrong' by the squire's son. Thora explained: 'I was the unfortunate result.' She had joyful memories of Jimmy Cooney, who was then the only 'coloured' man in Morecambe. 'When Jimmy died, the shock could not have been more heartfelt if the Clock Tower had fallen down. The funeral was one of the biggest I remember.'

Thora's grandfather, nicknamed 'Yallowman', was a trawlerman who sailed daily, except on Sunday, in a quest for shrimp. Several of her uncles were also fishermen. Huge, bearded men, like latter-day Vikings, they were recalled by Thora as 'fine, tough men, out in all weathers, always getting wet through'. Reared at a time when it was generally believed that the devil had work for idle hands, Thora was often put to work 'picking' (shelling) shrimp before she was allowed to go out to play. Encouraged not to dawdle or mope, she was scrubbing the front steps from the age of eight. She grew up with a curious impression of God, based on the appearance of her Uncle Robert, who with his seamless face and beard reminded some people of Jesus. When Thora prayed, it was to a God who wore a fisherman's gansey and had a cloth cap and a stick. At the age of 11, she mentioned this to her mother, who wisely observed, 'How do we know God doesn't look like that?' Chapel meant three services on Sunday, a Shrove Tuesday concert, potato pie suppers and the annual bazaar, preparations for which began weeks ahead of the event with the knitting of dish-cloths and making of lavender bags. As a teenager, Thora was familiar with the Monkey Walk (the Promenade) where young people 'clicked' and began their courtship.

She recalled winter days when the wind howling in from the west was of the 'lazy' variety, more inclined to cut through a person than go round. She would walk home to tea with a sou'wester on her head. On summer days, however, she might join holidaymakers on the shoreline, where, in the evening, the sky and sea seemed to blaze with red light from a low-slung sun. A fisherman just back from a trip might hand her a string of flatfish, saying, 'Does ta want a few flukes, joy?'

Flookburgh

Receiving its trading charters in 1278 and 1412, Flookburgh became the main fishing village on the Bay. Until 1798, when Winder Moor was enclosed, high spring tides swept right up to the little town. Subsequently there was a mile of windswept road between the fishermen's homes and the bay. Over 50 years ago it was common at Flookburgh, and also at Silverdale, Bolton-le-Sands, Baycliff and other points round the Bay, to see fishermen with horses and two-wheeled carts crossing the shining sands in the wake of the tide, seeking shrimp and shellfish. Early in the 20th century, before shrimping became popular, fishermen at Flookburgh were catching plaice, the weight of which averaged 'three to the pound'.

The name Flookburgh is said to be derived from the Anglo-Saxon *flooc*, relating to the flounder (*Platichthys flesus*), known locally as a fluke. Others claim that Flookburgh refers to Floki, a personal name, since it was pronounced 'Flokeburg' in 1246. The old church, a subsidiary of Cartmel, had 'neither minister or maintenance' in the mid-17th century; the dead were interred at Cartmel. The present commodious church, dedicated to St John the Baptist, was designed by the celebrated firm of Austin and Paley of Lancaster and constructed of stone from a quarry near the Home Farm at Holker. Queen Mary planted a hawthorn between the church and the road during a visit to Holker in September 1937. The church tower is topped by a weather vane in the form of a gilded fish. Some people claim it is a dolphin; what is certain, as an old chap said, is 'It isn't a fluke.'

16   *Flookburgh Church. On the weather vane is a gilded fish.*

Canon Taylor, author of *Cartmel, People and Priory*, was enthralled by the Flookburgh fishermen's use of a dialect that had a sprinkling of Old Norwegian words, similar to words used by Icelanders in the same trade of fishing:

> One of Flookburgh's younger men joined the Navy in 1939 and was sent as coastguard to the shores of Iceland. In his letters he stated that the Icelanders not only understood his home dialect but that he himself, when he went fishing with them, had no difficulty in understanding the terms they used.

Flookburgh's strategic importance as an intermediate stage on the oversands route to Ulverston was indicated by the presence of five inns in the main street: the *Royal Oak*, the *King's Arms*, the *Hope and Anchor*, the *Fishermen's Arms* and the *Crown* (where, it is said, Charles II was entertained to a feast of cockles). With the coming of the railway, however, the importance of Flookburgh as a halt for rest and refreshment declined; the village is also bypassed by the modern road to Barrow.

Local life is still coloured by tradition: memories endure of a time when clothing and pottery were sold around the old market cross. At Whitsuntide a fair would come to town, with swing-boats, hobby-horses, coconut shies and donkeys that carried children up and down the main street. At Flookburgh lived Old Tom Wilson, whose fame rested on the fact that he once caught a porpoise in a net set for much smaller prey. Tom brought the porpoise back to the village, cut it up and 'rendered it down' to make what he called 'porpoise oil'. People complained of the smell: 'There were a lot of funny smells in the village at that time but when Tom was making his porpoise oil, the place wasn't fit to live in.' Tom's oil was, of course, a cure for any ailment.

Fifty years ago horse-drawn carts could be seen propped outside the houses of the main street. In yards behind these houses the impedimenta of the fishing trade might be seen, including a wooden contraption with two handles known as a 'Jumbo', which was used for agitating the sand to bring up cockles. Another well-worn implement was the *craam*, a three-pronged, curved fork by which the cockles that surfaced were gathered up. Twenty years before that, a typical fisherman's cottage at Flookburgh would have been spartan in character. On the floor of lowly houses was 'just a bit of coconut matting, here and there'. A pegged rug was sometimes made from pieces of fabric cut from worn-out clothes and then deftly knotted on to a canvas base. Nearly all the houses had iron fireplaces that demanded a weekly application of black-lead for them to look well. A rack for drying clothes would be hung from the ceiling nearby. Oatcake, too, would be left to dry, the pieces looking for all the world like wash-leathers. On the wall above the high mantelpiece a framed picture or religious homily was usually displayed. Where the plain wooden furniture rested on a carpet, it was taken up at the start of the shrimp-picking season, or it was likely to become damp or damaged. An outbuilding held a boiler with an iron set-pot, used for boiling shrimps as well as doing the weekly wash.

When trade was slack or the weather poor a fisherman would sit for an hour or two 'knitting' nets. Those being repaired indoors were suspended from nails driven into a large beam or even into the walls. Nets made of cotton were dipped in the type of tar used for patching up a road. One lady remembered seeing an old bath half full of tar. A chap dropped a bundle of netting into it on a rope, gave the net a good soak, then pulled it out and let it drain. 'A net like that never really dried out. Even when you thought it was dry and took it to the Sands, you'd get clarted up.'

When Jack Manning's best friend began work as a farm labourer – he had left school at 14 and been hired at Ulverston – he was told by the man who took him on that he was not intending to give him a lot of money: 'If I did, thou'd only want time off to go and spend it.' With increasing affluence, a Flookburgh man lamented that his children would no longer sit around a table and pick shrimps. 'When we were kids, we'd earn a few pence doing this; then we'd go out and buy a few sweets. We were thrilled. Not now. You couldn't get some women to pick shrimps on a Saturday. They'd want to go off shopping.'

Adjoining the house at Flookburgh in which Jack Manning grew up was a stable for the horse. It was also the repository for homemade tackle. The *skel-booses* (barriers between stalls) were about six feet high and had been knocked up from old pieces of wood. The horses of Flookburgh were fed a good and varied diet: hay, oats and bran. Some families had a few acres of grassland and so there was a stock of hay for the winter. A local farmer mowed the grass. Fishermen who did not own land bought hay from farmers, bringing their own carts to collect it. Some fishermen rented small fields in which to graze their horses. When the author visited Flookburgh in the 1950s no less than 38 of the 40 horses stabled there were engaged in the fishing industry.

In the early 1900s horses were bought at the fairs held at Kendal, Lancaster and Brough Hill (in the upper Eden valley). Though it was customary to buy a horse through a dealer, every fisherman was alert to a local bargain, such as a horse no

longer needed by a farmer or a redundant nag from a horse-tram at Morecambe. Old
Tom Wilson kept one horse until it was 19 years old; he then sold it at Ulverston to
a man who harnessed it to a milk-dray in town. Harry Cowperthwaite was leading
his outfit to the sands one day when another fisherman started a discussion on the
price of horses. 'How much did you give for yon?' he demanded from Harry. 'Three
pun [pound] ten,' was the reply, 'an' I couldn't have got a better hoss than this if I'd
sung an old song.'

By the 1950s the fishermen owned bigger, stronger horses, most of them standing
at 16 hands. A good horse was vital to the fishing routine and across the flats of
Morecambe Bay would come shouts of encouragement: 'Goo' lad, goo' lad.' If a
fisherman had a good sound animal he would trust his life with it. Occasionally a
horse was swallowed up in a 'soft spot' or trapped by the tide. The author was told
that the body of one luckless animal was washed up on the Irish coastline.

Sand work was hard on horses, though the salt water was said to improve their
joints. 'There was never a poor horse to be seen on the Bay.' To be able to haul a

17   *Flookburgh village had its own market charter.*

load of half a ton of cockles a horse must be well shod; on the sands horseshoes, scoured by sand, had a life of nine or 10 months. 'Nails had to fit flush with the shoe. Horses working without shoes had feet so badly scoured the blood flowed.' A fisherman's high regard for his horse is illustrated by the care he took of it when the horse was idle for an hour or two during a cockling trip. If the wind were chill, he would remove the horse from the shafts, tip the cart up and tether the horse in its lee to cheat the cold wind. A Flookburgh man who had a mired horse began digging with a spade and found that *sipings* (water seeping into the hole) were troublesome. The horse made a special effort 'when it got a bit o' watter in its eye' and struggled free, although it was 'all cramped up. Off it set, in its tin-pot way, for home. It didn't want to know me for quite a while. Then it got its confidence back.'

18 *Potting shrimps at Flookburgh, north of the Bay.*

Making carts suitable for use on the Bay occupied two joiners at Flookburgh and two at nearby Cark. The carts were similar to those used on a farm, standing well off the ground, with two large wheels that reduced the drag in water. Some fishermen fitted rubber tyres to their wheels and reported that they ran better on the sands when laden. As the number of joiners declined, replacement carts were bought at farm sales. According to one of the Flookburgh men, one abandoned cart was so robust that it washed up, undamaged, on Chapel Island. Horses were succeeded in the role of drawing carts by tractors of the old type (one that might be driven in salt water without exposing its 'electrics'). The exhaust was turned upwards and wider mudguards were fitted. A trailer used by a fisherman at Baycliff had been adapted from an Austin 16 motor chassis. There were rather more *sieges* (mirings) with tractors than with horses; a tractor engine would start vibrating and, before a man could look round, the tractor would be sinking. Other tractors, with lines, would be summoned to free it. 'Latterly, they got to putting fifty gallon barrels on for buoyancy; they seemed to get away with that.'

In the days before refrigeration no one 'followed the sands' at weekends. Any fish caught then would not keep until Monday. Jessica Lofthouse, visiting Flookburgh, heard of women bound for the skears who carried their infant children in their shawls. Small girls were taught how to make nets: 'Every little lass had to knit so many meshes of a net afore she were let out to play. Later on, lasses and young women could turn out fine knitted ganseys for the menfolk.' Fisherfolk were adaptable, Flookburgh's inhabitants becoming preoccupied with trading when men began hawking cockles and fluke.

Then one or two of them arranged for herrings to be sent to them, adding to the variety. They also started to sell some of their garden produce. Then we had a fruit chap or two come – wholesale fruiterers – and before long there were 30 men selling produce. Some of them used old Austin cars, adapted for carrying goods.

Some Flookburgh men who retailed cockles were 'odd bag men', who toured with horses and carts, cockles being among the variety of produce they had for sale.

In the late 1940s a scarcity of cockles to the north of Morecambe Bay led William Robinson (Cedric's father) and Jim Benson to leave Flookburgh and seek new grounds near Silverdale, to which they travelled by rail. Good beds were found, so they returned with horses and carts to exploit them; they would stay overnight to avoid wasting too much time in travel. As they worked the cockle beds near Bolton-le-Sands and at Hest Bank, men they had never met opposed them. William recalls: 'One of them thought he owned the grounds. He very nearly did. He was a big strapping man!'

Experience led fishermen to become weather-wise. A recent heavy downpour could help at a river, for instance, causing the water to spread out and making the crossing easier. Difficulties arose if a *gullet* (a deep channel) was formed. The fishermen knew deep holes scoured by an incoming tide as *melgraves*; these varied from a depth sufficient to swallow up a man to just a few inches of the sloppy sand that filled them at the ebb. It was as well for a fisherman to know the notorious soft spots. A dyke near Humphrey Head, which was generally known as Holy Well Dyke ('Ally Well to a fisherman'), was difficult to negotiate. On one occasion a man

struck in wi' t'hoss' sooner than he should have done. He'd always claimed that his horse was a good one and 'would swim i' watter wi' just its lugs [ears] out'. This time, as the horse swam, the baskets floated from the cart and were washed away.

Another good horse was owned by David Wilkinson of Baycliff, who had his horse-drawn cart at the 'outscar' one wild day. On the return journey he snuggled down within the cart to cheat the weather and gave the horse its head; the horse unerringly returned to just the right place on the shore.

In a blizzard a curious illusion affected the bay: whichever way the fisherman looked, the snow appeared to be approaching him. If snow settled on the high banks it formed *snow broth* (mush) in shallow water. In a cold snap, ice floes drifting in the estuary gave the bay an Arctic flavour. The tide pushed some of the floes against the railway viaducts, prompting the company to set men to work at night, breaking up the ice with long poles. In winter fishermen walked rather than rode to the sands to avoid being *starved* (chilled). Before the days of waterproof clothing, men and women wore gabardine coats that were, at least, showerproof, but, 'if you were out there on a wet day you got soaked to the skin. If the sun came out, your clothes would dry on your back.'

Fog was the worst meteorological hazard for these people. Generations of fisherfolk ventured on to the bay without compasses and with limited visibility; trains rumbling across viaducts acted as guides as to the direction to take. Men on the Morecambe shrimping boats would shout to one another. One man cried out, 'It's clear up there,' pointing to a patch of blue sky. The reply was: 'Aye, and one day I'm going that way – God willing.' While shrimping with his son at night, a Flookburgh fisherman chose

19   *William Robinson, of Flookburgh. His son, Cedric, is now the Sands Guide (see p.13).*

to walk in front of the tractor to report on the quicksands, using a torch to signal to his son if a change of course were necessary.

A shrimper working eight miles from shore used to drive slowly, leaving deep imprints of the tractor tyres in the sand and mud. When fog gathered he used the tracks as his route back home and arrived at the exact spot where he had left dry land. Jack Manning, who normally worked alone, ventured out in 'wind, rain, fog, snow or whatever'. Having consulted a tide-table, he had the fisherman's ready knack of knowing how long the tide-free conditions would last in any part of the Bay. A compass was not reliable when using metal tractors and trailers; Jack nevertheless carried one of impressive size with a luminous face.

The fishermen were superstitious. On 17 March the most credulous would leave their clogs at the edge of the flanking marsh and advance across the sand barefoot, believing that on that date St Patrick had thrown a stone into the water and made it warmer. Cedric Robinson, who was reared at Flookburgh, encountered a sudden storm while leading a party of visitors across the sands to Chapel Island, in the estuary of the Leven. The walk began at Sandgate, in glorious weather. 'We set off wearing next

20 *Richard Burrow, a fisherman of Arnside, pictured wearing a gansey.*

to nothing. I was a little more sensible and carried a jersey over my arm. When we began the return walk, it was still a beautiful day.' A quarter of a mile out, Cedric heard a noise like an approaching tide, or a steam train on the Furness line. A storm was coming up the bay. 'The rain that hit us was like bullets, fast and fierce. All the marks left in the sand had been rubbed out. What had been dry sand suddenly became about two inches of sodden sand. Everything merged into one.' There were flashes of lightning in the murk. Cedric blew his whistle

> but it didn't make much difference, for we had broken up into three groups, each holding hands, walking head down. What had seemed like an age was only a matter of minutes. The storm passed. I blew the whistle again. We all got together – and talked about our frightening experience.

Back at the house in Cart Lane, Cedric's wife had watched the storm in comfort whilst washing clothes. 'I hung them out to dry. One moment, the washing was limp. The next moment it was being blown high in the air. I could hardly get it off the line.'

Three

HARVESTS OF THE BAY

In a television documentary Morecambe Bay was referred to as 'a wet Sahara'. Yet, although it may appear desolate, especially under low cloud, the Bay abounds with unseen life: molluscs, crustacea and annelid worms. George Mount, of Morecambe, claimed that one of his ancestors was the only man who had caught a halibut in Morecambe Bay. He towed the fish for almost five miles and landed it at Heysham. On the following morning the great fish was transported to Preston by donkey and cart. When George sold the halibut, he bought some coal and carted this back to Morecambe.

Of commercial interest are the cockles, mussels, shrimp and fluke that inhabit the Bay. The keen eye of a fisherman notices the *dawks* (feeding holes) or *shellings* (droppings) of fluke. At times the massed cockles are heard 'singing', a faint sound that has been compared to the pattering of light rain. Morecambe owed much of its wealth to mussels collected at the skears. E. Abercrombie, writing about the Cartmel peninsula, left us a striking word picture of the folk who made a living from the sands:

At every turn of the tide long lines of shrimp carts, with their mettlesome shire horses setting the pace, go rattling and lurching down all the lanes leading to the sea by Sandgate, Chanon Winder and Humphrey Head. They pass so far out on to the estuary that they become merged and lost in the gleam of wet sands and water and are seen only as a thin, intermittent black line on the horizon, returning hours later, heavily laden with their dripping harvest.

21 *Woman gathering cockles, an arduous occupation.*

On the bountiful Bay, and the tidal reaches of the rivers flowing into it, a *balk* was the oldest method of catching fish in bulk. At the dawn of the 20th century, at least 15 sets of balks were being operated between Cockersand and

Silverdale. Dr F.W. Hogarth, an authority on the Bay, theorised that the first such traps were erected by Celtic folk and that the Romans would have encouraged this local industry. Monks from local monasteries knew how to operate *balks* and almost certainly made technical improvements to them.

The ground plan of a *balk* made a huge 'V', with the open end landwards. The ingenious traps were set on a sloping beach so that when the open end was out of water at the ebb, the point of the 'V' was still in some six or seven feet. As the length of the arms was, in many cases, over 300 yards, a slope of at least one in 150 was required at right angles to the run of the tide. This requirement was not met very easily. Lengths of hazel and osier were wound between the stakes to form a compact basketwork wall on each side. Only stakes of ash or oak were able to withstand the continual strain of strong tides. Large rocks were backed along the outside of each arm to help. Two strong stakes marked the point of the 'V'; they were set far enough apart for a fisherman to be able to squeeze through. If the arms were correctly set, a shoal of fish entering the open end on the ebb tide would slowly make their way along the inside of one of the arms without being alarmed. When they began to feel trapped, the frantic fish would pass through a gap that appeared to lead to open water but, instead, ended in the 'cage', where the fish were confined by netting. Caught in this contraption, they remained stranded in pools when the tide ebbed.

Morecambe Bay Shrimp

The Bay is popularly associated with shrimp, the season for which extended 'from March until the onset of the first frosts', when the survivors left the Bay; a few might still be caught 'off Blackpool and the Mersey'. Shrimping came into its own at Morecambe after 1850 with the opening of urban markets following the arrival of the railway.

22 *Horse and cart fishermen heading out from Flookburgh.*

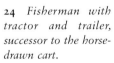

23 *Fisherwoman with horse and cart. Ashore, women 'picked' the boiled shrimps.*

24 *Fisherman with tractor and trailer, successor to the horse-drawn cart.*

The fleet of nobbies was enlarged and local people were employed in picking shrimp. The trawlermen took an early tide; in the absence of refrigeration, any shrimp caught had to be processed on the same day and placed on one of the late trains so as to arrive fresh at the inland markets. Shrimp were taken from the Ulverston Channel, from points off Silverdale and from below Heysham Head. The Lune Deeps, however, were too deep for shrimping in the Morecambe style.

The shrimp (*Crangon vulgaris*) can be found off Grange and Canal Foot, but mainly below Heysham on one hand and Chapel Island on the other. Freshly caught shrimp are grey and partly transparent. The first task was cleaning the catch and disposing of trawled-up rubbish, which was handled with care to avoid contact with the lesser weever, a venomous fish. Acceptable shrimp were riddled, washed and boiled on board, using a coal-fired boiler known as a 'talligoram', which held from eight to 12 gallons of water. Having been boiled in sea water, the shrimp were dunked in the sea to cool and harden. Meanwhile, the hot water was also used to heat up a drink carried in a billycan, and for cleaning up the boat.

25   *Morecambe nobbies – trawlers built by the Crossfield family at Arnside.*

On a short, sharp November day in 1969 the author met Dick Woodhouse of Morecambe, who had then been fishing from trawlers for over 50 years. His boat, *Kelpie*, was one of a fleet that returned up the Ring Hole Channel to moorings off the South Pier. Dick was the last of his family to venture into the Bay for shrimp, a sack of which would be his reward for an arduous few hours' fishing. On the day we met, Dick left Morecambe at 4 a.m. with the last of the ebb tide. A westerly wind made the sea lively, although conditions were marginally better than when wind and waves were contrary. In Morecambe Bay, banks and channels mean that the shortest distance between two points as the tide ebbs rarely runs in a straight line. Dick single-handedly covered four and a half miles to reach an area below Heysham harbour. It was still dark when he began to fish, and not until 7 a.m. was the daylight strong enough to see anything in fine detail. Dick was fond of saying, 'Some people are born daft, and I think I was one of them.' The tight little community of fisherfolk associated people with their boats: Richard Braid had the *Alice Alan* and Sam Baxter was the proud owner of *Girl Helen*, a modern boat.

A Morecambe woman with vivid memories of domestic life in the 1930s recalled that her dad, having boiled his shrimp on board, put them in sacks, cooled them by dipping the sacks in the sea and, on reaching home, tipped the shrimp into buckets. These were in turn deposited in smaller quantities on a large pine table, around which sat the pickers. As they deftly removed the husks, these ladies chatted or listened to the wireless. The shrimp went into enamel bowls; the husks were discarded in 'slough buckets', from which they would be tipped on to the shore for the benefit of the gulls. In the old days, picking shrimp was a regular weekday activity. A good picker could deal with a pound and a half of shrimp an hour, though in early times it became customary to measure rather than weigh shrimp; a volume of three *mollinge* equalled one stone. Two experts at Morecambe were said to have picked 1,128,000 shrimp in 12 months.

The method of shrimping differed greatly on the northern shore of the Bay, where men would work with hand nets; this occupation evolved to the stage where a horse-drawn cart drew a *shank* (conical net) through the water. The net, of half-inch mesh, was attached to a wooden frame of 12 to 13 feet. The bottom part of the frame was usually made of pitch pine so that it would hug the bottom of the channel, the top part being of softer wood such as hazel or ash. Ropes attached the net to the cart. When the pitch pine encountered the shrimp, they leapt over the bar and landed in the net. A Flookburgh man was almost guaranteed to get a few shrimp around 20 March at the start of a new season. Shrimping at night was sometimes practised; the working time was reduced by the long journeys to and from the shore between tides.

In the early part of the 20th century, the main difficulty on the northern shore of Morecambe Bay was selling shrimp. In the 1950s Messrs Young, one of the oldest firms in the seafood business, established a factory at Cark, where picked shrimp were cooked in hot butter and the molten mixture ladled into screw-top wax cartons. When the contents had set, the lids were screwed into place and the cartons wrapped in greaseproof paper. After orders had been met, the remaining shrimp were frozen, to be used during the leaner months of the year.

26 *Unpicked shrimp, a long-standing Morecambe Bay delicacy.*

The shrimp-pickers of Flookburgh were a gregarious lot, laughing, chattering and gossiping the hours away. The still living shrimps were put in a cast-iron boiler in an outhouse, which brightened their colour. Fishermen's wives contrived to have the water on the boil as soon as the menfolk arrived home. The special character of the shrimp harvested at Flookburgh meant that they were boiled in fresh, rather than salt, water.

> You always gave the missus a good idea of what time you would arrive; if it was warm clashy weather, the sooner the shrimps were boiled the better it was. If they were a bit on the dead side they were not good to pick.

Shrimp were boiled up several times. If one or two were tested, and found to be a bit on the 'tuggy' side, they would be left 'on the boil' a little longer.

Before hygiene laws were introduced boiled shrimp were spread on hessian sacking lying on the ground. Thereafter they were placed on trays standing on a raised surface. Shrimp used to be scalded for cleanliness after they had been picked. It made them look better but the resulting flavour was not so good. At Flookburgh, a lady started with 13 lb of 'shrimps in the shell', enough to fill two good buckets, and within an hour had produced 3¼ lb of 'shrimp meat'. This feat was possible because she was handling large shrimp in good condition. Elsewhere, a good picker produced from 1½-2 lb of picked shrimp in an hour.

Shortly after the Second World War, Bob Burrow, a fisherman living at Bolton-le-Sands, introduced an ex-Army DUKW to the Sands. On its way to the shrimping grounds this vehicle took less than a quarter of the normal time. Being amphibious,

it could draw the net up a channel, filling it quickly with shrimp. Two further trips were undertaken; the shrimping area widened in consequence. By the 1940s, shrimp was being potted with unsalted butter and spices.

At Flookburgh a firm was set up so that local fishermen could market their own products. The company had been formed in 1959, with an office and workroom standing beside the Marsh Road. A score of local families were originally involved but by 1975 the number had dwindled to about a dozen. The firm processed between 10 and 12 tons of shrimp a year, which were delivered to the workplace already picked. Mr C.F. Bartle, the manager, also bought shrimp from other parts of the Cumbrian coast, even from Wales.

Some thirty years have elapsed since Morecambe Trawlers, once a successful marketing organisation, was closed down, though with the demise of Fleetwood's last

27 Les Butler with a tray of Morecambe Bay shrimps.

deep-sea trawler in 1982 the Morecambe men were able to supply the local market with fish, as they had done so many years before. Morecambe Bay Shrimp are still available under that name.

COCKLES

Joseph Lucas, an 18th-century chronicler, wrote that cockles found in Morecambe Bay were 'so excellent in their kind, and so much preferable to those on the East Shore of England that they are carried 60 or 70 Mile Eastward'. He mentioned 'cockle skears', where cocklers trod or ran over the sand, 'which Motion works them [the cockles] up to the Top of ye Sand'. A Flookburgh nonagenarian told Jessica Lofthouse, the author, that she had begun cockling in the 1860s, at the age of five: 'There was no schooling for the likes of us.' As a newly-wed she had gone out on the sands with her husband in a shrimp-cart. 'When childer came, why, I fastened a baby in my shawl and no harm came.'

A good cockler would spot the small breathing holes of the shellfish. Near such holes one might find a moss-like growth. Into play came the *craam*, and in one graceful movement cockles were lifted up and dropped into a basket. The fact that cockles might be lured to the surface by stamping, to agitate soft sand, led Peter Butler, a Flookburgh lad, to design the aforementioned 'Jumbo'. He had been using an 'empty horse tub' to coax the shellfish to the surface. 'Jumbo', the refined design, was a large flat board on which two or three handles were set at right angles. The baseboard was four feet six inches long, one foot two inches wide and half an inch thick. Four uprights of lighter wood supported two handles that were grasped by the cockler, who was then able to rock the base.

28   A 'Jumbo', *devised locally for bringing cockles to the surface of the sand.*

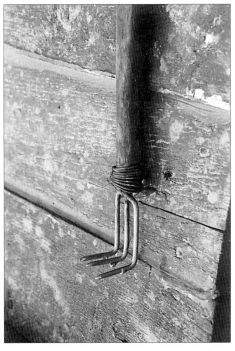

29   A craam, *used for collecting cockles on the Sands.*

30   *Morecambe Bay
cockles. Vast quantities
were once despatched
from Cark station.*

Cocklers worked hard in Holy Week to fulfil orders for the Good Friday market in Manchester. Before the building of the railway, cockles from the banks below Flookburgh were carted to Hest Bank for despatch to Preston by canal boat. Flookburgh men on the northern shore eventually began despatching their cockles from Cark railway station; in 12 months in 1902-3 Cark handled 741½ tons of cockles, 171 of mussels and 6¾ of fluke, for which a special train was needed. Horses and carts hurried across the sands to catch it. Prior to the First World War a train consisted of as many as 10 wagons. When the author visited Flookburgh in 1954, he saw a red-painted lorry collecting sacks of cockles. It left with a load of six tons, which was delivered to Lytham, where there was a plant for shelling, sterilising and bottling. The lorry was calling several times a week. By amazing good fortune, two bumper seasons at Flookburgh coincided with a dearth of cockles along other stretches of the Lancashire coast.

Just within living memory, cockles were selling at £6 or £7 a hundredweight; they fell to £3 a hundredweight – boiled. A sudden demand for cockles recently inflated the price to £1,000 a ton. Hundreds of people visited the best cockle beds. Tragedy occurred on 5 February 2004 when 21 Chinese cockle-pickers, having little knowledge of the whims of weather and tide, became trapped by a flow tide when they were several miles from the shore and were drowned. In August 2004 an estimated 140 cocklers were stranded by the tide while operating just off the coast of Newbiggin, near Ulverston. Local fishermen have been concerned at the indiscriminate nature of this operation, which has meant that juvenile cockles, on which the future of the industry depends, have been scooped up along with the mature shellfish. (A tempory ban on cockling has been imposed.)

Mussels

Mussels can be harvested in Morecambe from September to April. In its immature state a mussel (*Mytilus eduis*) drifts with the tides. In its mature state it is a filter-feeder, gradually rising on the beds of sediment that nourish it and settling on the skears. Whereas in Wales one might find giant mussels (ones that would make a worthy meal), at Heysham Skeers growth was not as rapid and the average mussel rarely exceeded two and three-quarter inches. Mussels were lifted from Jacky John Skeer, Bank Side Skeer and Knott End Skeer.

31   *A mussel bed off Foulney Island, near Barrow.*

FLUKE

The fluke frequents the estuaries, feeding on shellfish at high water. It has a white belly with brown on the topside, a tone that varies according to the nature of the seabed on which it rests. A familiar story told at Flookburgh relates that a visiting clergyman asked how many souls there were in the place. The word soul being misheard as 'sole', which is found in the lower part of the Bay, the reply given was: 'I don't knaw – but there's a terrible lot o' flukes.'

Dick Burrow, the last of Arnside's full-time fishermen, became a patient hunter of fluke which, spawning in deep water, swam up the estuaries in April and May to settle on the beds of tidal rivers with a thin covering of sand over them when the tide was out. A flow tide enabled them to swim to the sandbanks to feed on shellfish, and an observant fisherman like Dick would notice bits of shell they had ground up. He had a long purse-net that he lowered into the water from a boat, and by creating noise with a 'posser' he scared fish into the purse. Fluke were also caught at their feeding grounds on the sandbanks by setting up a 300-yd net which, being a 'fixed engine', might be left out for days. The fluke migrated with the first frosts, often in one night, to deeper water. Dick's cousins lower down the Bay sometimes netted so many fluke the nets might be flattened by the weight of fish. 'When this happens, we might as well give up fishing at Arnside, unless there are one or two mild days and a few fish get back.' Frank Benson, who combined the work of a fisherman with his duties as guide

32   *Whitebait, caught in fixed nets.*

to Leven Sands, set his nets near the rocks of Black Scar or Chapel Island, between which the river flowed. The fishermen hoped to reach their nets before the gulls could take first pick of the fish. Sometimes, if the nets were set on a high bank in wild weather, the stakes would be pounded by the waves and brought to the surface. After a 'blow' a fisherman might find his nets had vanished or, having been lifted, were hopelessly tangled.

A good fluke weighed about a pound – enough to provide someone with a meal. 'We fillet flukes now,' the author was told in the 1980s. 'This came in during the last 20 years when old Tom Wilson, of Flookburgh, started to sell filleted fluke from a basket, which he carried on his arm. He went round the villages.' In one outbuilding, which had no proper door, only slats such as a gate might have, a lady spent many hours filleting fish. It was terribly draughty, yet she sat there, on and off, for years, filleting fluke for her father. 'He'd hawk 'em round the village.' Folk used to smoke fluke by hanging them in the house chimney: 'That wouldn't go down well now.'

WHITEBAIT

Morecambe trawlermen were taking whitebait for years before fishermen north of the Bay decided it was worth netting them, which they did on the banks. Here an ebb tide moves more swiftly than in the channels; the whitebait net will float even when moored to a given spot. Luck as well as skill is needed to trap the shoaling fish. 'If there's a row of nets, one net might hold four stones of nice clean fish and the other nets could be virtually empty.'

The outbreak of war in 1939 led to a demand for home-produced food, which meant that fishing in Morecambe Bay throve as never before. Whitebait became popular. The monks of Furness almost certainly knew about whitebait, but for many years the fish had been ignored commercially. Whitebait was a winter harvest, caught between November and April, so it provided lucrative work at a normally quiet time. Nets were placed on high ground, where the ebb tide flowed more quickly, iron bars with ropes attached being sunk in the sand to act as moorings for the nets; for catching fluke, on the other hand, nets were attached to stakes. In the 1970s, whitebait at the Flookburgh factory was frozen immediately and marketed unprocessed, so only packing the fish was involved. Fishermen on the north coast of Morecambe Bay were then catching about thirty tons a year of this highly nutritious fish, which was deep-fried and served in high-class restaurants; local folk were inclined to eat this tasty food on toast.

Four

SEABORNE TRADE

An entry in the old Church Book of Cartmel for 1598 mentions the off-loading of 12 tons of 'sea-coales' at Grange. What are now obscure byroads heading northwards were then important links between coastal jetties and the hinterland. In some cases ships were unloaded as they lay on their sides at low tide. A boat that left Lancaster for America in 1676 was the first of many trading vessels that were financed by merchants such as William Stout, a Quaker, whose investment in the transatlantic trade caused it to burgeon. In 1700 the first ever shipment of cotton to reach England was put ashore at Sunderland Point, near the mouth of the Lune.

One enduring local legend is that of a Negro houseboy called Sambo, who died at Sunderland Point in 1736. His master, a ship's captain named Joshua Lawson, left him at Sunderland while attending to some business in Lancaster, intending to collect him later. The boy, thinking he had been deserted, pined away and died. In reality he was more likely to have been a victim of our cold, damp climate, having come from a hot country. Denied a Christian burial, he was interred some distance away. On his tombstone are the words: 'Then the Great Judge his approbation founds, Not on colour but on worth of heart.' Local people still put flowers on the grave.

Lancaster flourished under a Port Commission that, established in the 1740s, arranged for the construction of a quay and a customs house. After the link with Chester had been broken, the port had its heyday; Lancaster also controlled the trade at various creeks, including Angerton, Bardsea, Cartmel, Cockersands Abbey, Grange, Ireleth and Storth. Lancaster ships collected slaves in Africa and transported them to the West Indies, returning with sugars, rum, spices, fruit and tobacco. The local trade peaked in 1799, when 61 ships docked at Lancaster. The focus at that time was on war with France, a rival colonial power. Official sanction having been given to privateering, Captain Charnley became a local hero. In 1804 a desperate rearguard action, fought from his ship *Thetis* against the *Buonaparte*, saved the island of Dominica.

In 1711 an ore-smelting furnace had been established at Backbarrow, by the Leven. Several other furnaces were also built. The demand for charcoal, a product of the expansive deciduous woods, outstripped supply, so vast quantities of the rich haematite ore of Furness were shipped for processing elsewhere. Also being exported were copper ore, slate and timber.

At high tide Morecambe Bay saw the passage of ships of all types. Along the Furness shore, between the rivers Crake and Leven and down to the fine natural harbour of

33 *Lakeland slate, quantities of which were shipped from bayside jetties.*

Piel, 'mine floors' appeared for the reception of ore delivered in horse-drawn carts; it would be stored in these prior to shipment. 'Mine floors' existed at Penny Bridge, Hammerside Point, Conishead and Baycliff.

To the east of the bay, Arnside, Silverdale and Milnthorpe handled a wider variety of goods, and for a time the former two were in the business of importing iron ore for a furnace at Leighton Beck. When this closed, salt and coal became the main imports. Milnthorpe, renowned as the only seaport in Westmorland, was reached via the Kent estuary and a short, navigable stretch of the Bela river. Milnthorpe had no harbour as such; there was no quay and associated buildings were well dispersed. Some ships with goods for Milnthorpe off-loaded part of their cargoes at Grange so that they might 'clear the flatts'. With the building of a port at Glasson on the Lune, and its link by canal with Lancaster and Kendal, the port of Milnthorpe went into sharp decline.

J. Stockdale noted in 1872 that, 'for many years, vessels of the burden of 50 to 200 tons were built at Carke [Cark-in-Cartmel] … These vessels traded with countries up to the Baltic or with the then British possessions in America and the West Indies.' The flow tide surges through a narrow gap, now spanned by a railway bridge, and washes against faint traces of a wharf that, in pre-railway days, was used for tying up the flat-bottomed vessels that arrived with coal for local businesses.

Flookburgh achieved a measure of fame in the 18th century for its part in the smuggling and piracy that raged up and down the coast. Boats from the duty-free Isle of Man lay off Lenibreck Point and contraband was brought ashore concealed in the shrimp carts, to be despatched secretly over a wide area, including the remoter parts of Lakeland.

Greenodd was once a bustling port, and a reception point for copper mined in the Coniston area. The ore was transported down Coniston Water in barges to a jetty on the southern tip of the lake, where it was off-loaded into horse-drawn carts and transported to Greenodd's wharves and quays. These handled coal, pig-iron, saltpetre, brimstone, black-lead and limestone, in addition to slate and copper ore; imported goods included cotton, manufactured yarns, spirits, porter, oats and corn. Many industries flourished at Greenodd: George Postlethwaite had a lime-kiln; Richard Taylor Wood was a saddler; at I.B. Fell's saw mill, wood, both English and foreign, was cut up for the country joiners; there were also nail-makers and a tannery. It was also at Greenodd that William and Richard Ashburner, ship-builders, launched and fitted out the *Ann Rennison*, a schooner of more than 100 tons. William later transferred his activities to Barrow, while Richard went on to build the first two steamships used on Windermere.

Products of the Furness coppice woods, which make up one of the largest tracts of deciduous woodland in the England, were conveyed to Greenodd as yet another part of its extensive seaborne trade. The exports included hoops, brooms, baskets, rods, pit props, bobbins and cotton reels. In the early 18th century, with charcoal in short supply for processing ironstone, several Furness undertakings built furnaces in the well-wooded Western Highlands of Scotland. Backbarrow, the first concern to do this, was operating a furnace at Invergarry in 1737. As ships bringing ironstone could not get close to the site, the undertaking closed after about nine years. The industrialised valley of the Leven, between Newby Bridge and Greenodd, bustled with a variety of concerns. In 1908 Alfred Fell enumerated about thirty bloomeries in Furness, most of them in the Coniston area. This industry was to operate, with furnaces of increasing size, until the ore had been worked out and foreign ore was being imported. In Elizabeth I's reign restrictions were placed on the cutting of timber for charcoal. With the succession of James I, larger bloomery forges, in some cases using water power to drive bellows and trip hammers, came into operation at places that were given evocative names, among them Spark Bridge and Force Forge. More refined material was produced, but by about 1700, with a greatly increased demand for iron, both cast and forged, even larger furnaces were being operated.

The aforementioned furnace established at Backbarrow in 1711 came into being through the enthusiasm (and means) of William Rawlinson and several partners; it was the first of eight such 'orthodox' furnaces established in south Cumbria which plied the craft of flat-iron making, where the iron was carried in ladles across the road to the workshop. Then came the invention of the 'box-iron', a humble domestic appliance. John 'Iron-Mad' Wilkinson (1728-1808), who would revolutionise iron production at the start of the Industrial Revolution, began his working life with his father at Backbarrow.

At the end of the Seven Years' War, in 1763, Wilkinson senior and one of his sons 'went to the wall'. John Wilkinson was able to keep his business alive, partly by marrying a rich heiress, but also because his initiative and enterprise attracted capital. Before John Wilkinson's innovations, iron furnaces used leather bellows to obtain the draughts. He devised a greatly improved method involving tubular iron bellows that

34 *Charcoal-burning for local industries, including the gunpowder works.*

worked somewhat like a telescope. With the risk of denuding areas of woodland for charcoal, coke came into use. Wilkinson's great moment, however, came with his production of commercial iron that was light but strong. How he produced his special iron is a mystery, but it is possible that he made use of Dr Priestley's knowledge of the properties of oxygen; one of his daughters had married the great scientist. Wilkinson is credited with having owned the first iron-hulled craft, a barge used for transporting peats from the mosses down the Winster. He owned furnaces at Backbarrow, but his main works stood near Coalbrookdale in Shropshire. From them came the cast-iron parts for the world's first iron bridge, erected at a place that became known as Ironbridge, a mile from Coalbrookdale, in 1779.

The cutting of a ship canal at Ulverston in 1796 led to the rise of various industries there, ranging from paper-making to ship-building. The canal was described as the shortest, widest, deepest and straightest in Britain. In 1821, 259 vessels, equivalent to 13,960 tons, used it. From 1829, when a new warehouse was built, until 1844, the number of ships sailing from the Bay into town averaged 531, with a total tonnage of 35,009. Ulverston hummed with activity. Among the products available were edge tools, bar iron, spades, axes, rope candlewicks, ginghams, linen, cotton, flax, oilcloth and sackings; many of these local goods were exported via ship. An account written by John Kellett, timber merchant of Arrad Foot, a village now bypassed, recalled a spring morning in about 1848 when, aged eight or nine, he was in charge of two horses hauling a cartload of gunpowder to the canal. At that time it seemed to be full of workaday schooners. Coal represented half the material being off-loaded, so the workers had black faces and terrible thirsts, which they slaked with Barleycorn. This in turn led to quarrels and free fights.

Young John Kellett saw barge-like sailing ships known as Preston Flatts, each with a capacity of 50 tons and manned by a captain and mate. When a flatt had been emptied, prop-wood was taken aboard for the mines of Tarleton and Preston. The sailing ships visiting Furness ports also collected iron ore, sailing as far as the Dee and Mersey, Cardiff and Newport. Ironically, the two years of greatest activity,

35   *Charcoal-burner's hut, reconstructed at Hay Bridge, near Bouth.*

1845 and 1846, sounded the death knell for the canal. Some of the ships arriving at that time carried materials needed for the construction of the Furness Railway and the arrival of rail transport lessened the demand for seaborne goods. In 1864 the railway company bought the waterway. Although the canal was subsequently plugged, the skeletal remnant of a lock gate remains, spanning the water like a piece of futuristic art. With car parking space for visitors, Canal Foot now offers a view of the Leven railway viaduct, the blue-grey hills beyond, and the sparkling estuary. A tuft of trees rising above the sands marks out tiny Chapel Island.

Barrow had its introduction to industry early in the 18th century, when four jetties for shipping ore were built out into the channel that separated Barrow Island from the mainland. In 1863 Barrow Island was purchased from the Duke of Buccleuch. Later an Act was obtained allowing Furness to create the Buccleuch

36 *Jack Allonby of Spark Bridge, an authority on the making of charcoal.*

and Devonshire Docks, which involved closing the Barrow Channel. There followed the creation of the Ramsden and Cavendish Docks. Spoil was dumped to extend Barrow Island. The main shipments through the new system of docks were pig-iron and steel rails. Edwin Waugh, our intrepid Victorian traveller, arriving in Barrow by train, noticed long strings of carriages going by. They were 'heavily laden with the rich iron ore of Furness'. He was told that mines in the district were annually producing between 700,000 and 800,000 tons of the finest ore in England. Yet, 30 years before, old Captain Barrow (cousin to Sir John Barrow, of the Royal Navy) had transported all the Furness ore in one small vessel.

Charcoal produced in the coppice woods was used in products that were exported by sea. Among these were agricultural baskets known as *swills*. Those who made them wore fustian waistcoats with sleeves to protect them against the cold, for they spent most of their working lives seated. Sections of young oak trees were boiled in a 15 foot wide iron tank. The swill-maker would then *rive* them into strips known as *spells*. Hazel formed the *bool* or frame of the swill. The swill-making industry waned with the decline in the coppice woods. To sustain such activity, but mainly to provide charcoal for industry, the woods were intensely coppiced, a tract being felled every 15 years or so. The season for 'winter wood' ended on 5 April, and from early May to early July, when the sap was running, oak was cut for the bark which was sold to tanners (the word *tan* originally referred to a young oak tree). Bark was tied up in bundles and stored against the time when, in a wet spell, it might be chopped into two-inch lengths. The

37 *Jack Allonby and a partially completed besom.*

38 *Coppice wood, the basis of many woodland crafts.*

process of making charcoal was simple. Heat was used to reduce wood to carbon. Just enough oxygen was introduced to burn the wood without flame.

Juniper, which flourished on hillsides, made the best charcoal for gunpowder, which was needed by the iron industry and also for military purposes. Juniper became scarce through both the activities of the burners and being grazed by sheep. The Coucher Book of Furness Abbey has many entries relating to colliers, or charcoal-burners. Cartmel Fell chapel was dedicated to St Anthony, whose varied patronages include charcoal-burners. Tyson, a relatively common Lakeland surname, is a corrupt form of Anthony. Iron smelted using charcoal rather than coal was most free from sulphur and could therefore be toughened and made into steel more easily.

The sites where charcoal was burnt had various names – *pitsteads*, *pitrings*, *cole-pitts* or *cole-pots*. Circular traces of such activity are common in Furness. Mary C. Fair, the Lakeland historian, related that when she was young she remembered seeing charcoal-burners at work. Filmy, blue-grey smoke rose from their smouldering pile. She admired the skill and deftness with which *saying* was carried out, *sayes* being flat dishes containing the water dashed against any pitstead about to burst into flame. Miss Fair was impressed by the accuracy shown by a man with a long-handled shovel throwing finely sifted earth just where it was wanted. At the start of a new burning season, the men first moved the *cover* (new vegetation) from the pits. Hurdles used to control the amount of air reaching a pitstead were re-backed with bracken.

'Coalers' of Furness practised their arduous, uncomfortable craft within living memory. We remember the names of some of them: Jack Clarke, Jack Martindale, Tommy Lammas, Billy Wilson and George Mashiter. During the coaling season, a man might set off from home on Sunday evening or Monday morning, returning for a brief spell the following weekend. Alice Black, reared at Near Sawrey, was the daughter of a charcoal-burner who had been familiar with the craft from his eighth birthday and who worked until his mid-sixties. He spent most of his life in the woods, so that the family saw him only on Sunday. On a weekday, he set off for work at 4 a.m. and, during the summer, it might be 10 p.m. before he arrived back at home, although much of the time was taken up by walking to and from his workplace. He was paid 18 shillings a week. When there was a 'burn' he arrived back home once a fortnight for food, which he usually kept in an old tin trunk whilst in the woods. Some of the charcoal-burners put boxes of clay pipes in the pits. When the charcoal was removed the pipes were considered to be well-seasoned and had increased in value.

Jack Allonby of Spark Bridge said, 'You could tell a charcoal-burner by his dark complexion. And his eyes looked watery; he was always among smoke.' Jack recalled that fustian was popular

39 *Edward Hughes, basket-maker. The basket was known as a* swill.

for clothing – for jacket, waistcoat and trousers. His shirt was made of flannel. Some workers wore clogs but woodmen preferred good shoes with the addition of leather leggings, which prevented sawdust from filtering into the footwear. 'Nearly all the shoes were hand-sewn. If your feet let you down, you really were down.' The coalers chewed or smoked black twist and dined mainly on ham and bacon brought from home. 'Father kept two pigs especially for coaling-time.' Bread was kept in a large tin into which mice could not nibble, since the warmth of a cabin attracted rodents. The countryside yielded rabbits, but adders could be a nuisance. Jack's grandmother once left a pan containing a little milk outside her home; when she went to collect it, several adders were found inside drinking the milk. Grandmother promptly put the lid on the pan and set it on the kitchen fire.

Jack was familiar with the traditional charcoal-burner's living cabin, which was of the type used by countless generations of men in Furness. Men who were operating up to five miles from home needed such durable accommodation. It was vital when a pit was burning that it should not be left untended, because no part of it could be allowed to burst into flame. A cabin consisted of a low circular wall with an internal diameter of 12 feet. The wall, made without a dab of mortar, was breached in two places to allow for a doorway and a hearth. When the timber superstructure had been covered with sods it resembled a wigwam. The timbering was coppice wood that had been hewn locally using axe and billhook. The bark was removed from the three main stays and these stays were tied together at the top. Sods were cut using a special, long-shafted turf-spade, and set in such a way that they slightly overlapped each other, thus keeping out the weather. 'Real old fell-sods were the best. Sods from ground that had been limed let the rain through!' Sodding took at least two days, the area to be covered being 80 square yards.

A cabin had to be well aired to keep fungi at bay. The substantial hearth was fitted with a sheet of metal to deflect flames from the roof. A draught from the doorway kept the fire in good heart and with the chimney at the highest point the smoke cleared the area. Building a chimney was 'a particular job', which could, if not done correctly, lead to the cabin filling with smoke. Rushes were sometimes laid on the bare earth; two rough beds were the major furnishings. To make a bed, four pronged sticks were driven into the ground and poles stretched between them. Birch *chat* (branches) were spread across the poles. Smaller shelters that were built close to the pitsteads lacked the low wall.

The men who attended a 'burn' were on duty by night as well as day and therefore seldom undressed. They 'simply lay down with their clothes on'. If a coaler was lucky, said Jack Allonby, a farmer gave him some straw with which to stuff the pillows. Some men spread large rugs over them when they prepared to sleep, but most relied on the new bags issued by the manager of the gunpowder factory at Backbarrow to hold charcoal. When more bags were received, the first batch was used for this purpose. Despite the austerity of the huts, George Davison, a builder who lived at Stock Farm, Nibthwaite, was so proud of the cabins he built that he preferred them to living in a conventional house. Even after being taken to hospital, where he later died, he retained fond memories of his woodland cabin.

40 *Swill-making equipment.*

When men began to clean off the pitsteads, levelling them up, soil that had passed through a half-inch riddle was heaped up to be used when an airproof layer had to be maintained. Stacking the wood was done methodically, with a stout piece of wood set vertically at the centre, and other pieces, known as *billets*, set at varying angles to form a cone about six feet in height. The central stake was then removed and replaced by dry twigs, which were positioned via a temporary hole. A fire was then kindled in the void. The slow burn had began. The charcoal pit method of production was abandoned by about 1927. It was succeeded by a retort method, which was used during the 1930s and later revived; it is still in limited use today.

Coalers took a variety of musical instruments with them to the woods: fiddle, concertina, mouth organ and jew's harp. Playing these was a satisfying occupation. When Jack Allonby was a lad, a sport frowned upon by the adults but enjoyed by children was racing round a smoking pit. A runner had to hold his breath or he would breath in dank and heavy smoke. So thick was the smoke that a lad would sometimes run into the pit.

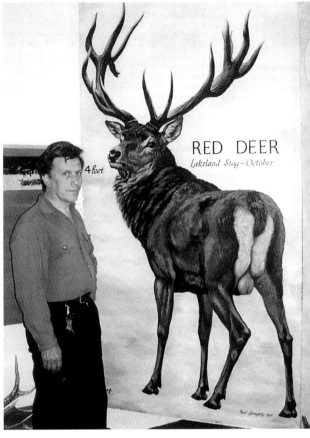

41 *Study of a Furness red stag, painted for the museum at Hay Bridge nature reserve.*

The men were paid an agreed rate per dozen bags of charcoal delivered to Backbarrow. 'There were set prices for coaling and carting.' Jack's father worked on his own. He bought standing coppice at a fixed rate per acre. In 1907 he felled some woodland that made 15 tons of charcoal, for which he was paid at the rate of £10 a ton.

Another local export by sea was gunpowder, which came from a factory at Low Wood, on the banks of the Leven. In 1796 this remote area had a handy source of good quality charcoal, and the tidal Leven could be used for the barges that transported the gunpowder in barrels and casks to the port of Greenodd for transhipment. Most varieties of coppice could be used to make the barrels; sycamore was one of the exceptions. A full barrel held 100 lb of gunpowder. Quarter-barrels were generally used for the home trade. Gunpowder intended for export to Nigeria and the Gold Coast was sent in small casks or kegs fitted with *smarts* (hoops made of hazel saplings). The hooper used a wooden contraption called a *mare* when splitting the end of the smart. The gap created was pressed on to a peg and the hammer was twisted to split the strip of wood lengthwise. Rounding off the hoop, using a broad pulley wheel, and tying into a bundle, were further adroit movements that made hooping a craft. In 1800 over 2,000

42   *Lakeland red stag 'roaring' during the autumnal rut.*

sacks of charcoal were used in 11 months at Low Wood. Sixty years later, working on the wise principle of dispersal, Low Wood had 14 separate mills in operation. The powder was moved in horse-drawn wagons on narrow-gauge rail tracks. Copper shoes were fitted to the hooves of the horses. With such a hazardous business, it was inevitable that a 'big bang' would occur, which it did in 1863, killing six men. After several changes of management, the enterprise closed down in 1935.

Coastal shipping flourished until, in 1857, the Brogden family completed the outer ring of Cumbrian railways with the Ulverston-Carnforth stretch, which linked up with the Lancaster-Carlisle section. A visitor to Sunderland Point in the last days of sail might have been surprised to see a sailing ship resting on the foreshore. *John & William*, a 70-ton 'flat', one of the last of many to operate on the north-west coast, had not run aground but, with a specially-strengthened hull, had arrived at high water to off-load a cargo of roadstone. Relieved of her cargo, the vessel would float off at the next high tide. At about the turn of the century a steam-driven coaster with a wooden hull delivered another load of roadstone to Sunderland Point. This time the cargo was off-loaded by steam-powered crane. Steam-driven ships were supplanting those under sail. The last boat to use the Morecambe Steamboat Company's pier at Grange, before the bay silted up, was the *Sunbeam* in 1910.

Five

FURNESS RAILWAY

In the summer of 1837 George Stephenson, an audacious engineer, was asked to survey the route of a proposed railway northwards from Preston. The requirement was for a quick route to Carlisle, the gateway to Scotland. Instead of drawing a line between two points and trying to fit the line into local topography, he opted for a low-level route across Morecambe Bay between Poulton and Humphrey Head. The railway track would be set on embankments, thus reclaiming the bay for farming. At the time, his proposal had the advantage of opening up one of the most remote parts of the country, to which access was impeded by the broad estuaries of the Kent and Leven. It would also be a boon to the mining industry, which had seen rapid expansion in the 18th century. The haematite iron ore was being exported by sea, much of it via John Rennie's ship canal at Ulverston, which was then the regional capital. A Parliamentary Commission, however, ignored the recommendations of both Stephenson and John Hague, another brilliant engineer, preferring the hilly but more direct Shap route at about double the cost.

The rise to prosperity of the extractive and iron industries in Furness and West Cumberland led to the construction of mineral lines. Originally the Furness Railway had humble aspirations: to improve transport facilities at a time when iron ore was shipped to South Wales by way of Barrow, a hamlet with about a score of houses on the south-western shore of Furness, sheltered by Barrow Island and Walney. By the early 1840s, when the tonnage of ore had reached 40,000 a year, a railway was proposed and given enthusiastic support by the two main landowners, the Duke of Buccleuch and William Cavendish, Earl of Burlington, whose commercial interests extended to slate quarries as well as ironstone mines. In a commissioned report, James Walker, a notable civil engineer, envisaged 14 miles of railway constructed at an estimated cost of £100,000. Initially horses would work the system, with the prospect of using locomotives when desired.

The Furness Railway Company's plans were approved by Parliament, without dissent, in May 1844. The proposed system would extend from Kirkby slate quarries to Barrow, with branches connecting Dalton and Rampside. Before a rail had been laid it was decided to extend the Rampside branch to a pier on Roa Island so that ships might be berthed at any state of the tide. The railway, passing close to Furness Abbey, upset William Wordsworth, the Lakeland poet. He would have thought more kindly of it had he known that the original proposals were for a line right through the ruins!

43   *The 0-6-2 tank engine No.98 at Grange-over-Sands in about 1910. Locomotive livery would be Indian red, with blue and white coaches. Apart from the train, the scene has changed little today. (Courtesy of the Cumbrian Railways Association Shillcock Collection.)*

The Furness Railway was officially opened in 1846. The appointment of 23-year-old James Ramsden as locomotive superintendent, and subsequently as secretary and manager of the company, ensured its successful development. Four locomotives, designed by Edward Bury, were conveyed to Furness on the decks of tugboats. Just how the locomotives arrived was recounted by Thomas Fisher in *A Popular History of Barrow-in-Furness*:

> When the tide was at a height that left the deck of the tug-boat on a level with the pier, we got to work, put a line of rails from the pier on to the boat, got the engine placed on the rails and made fast our rope and chains on to it; and then with a long pull and a strong pull and a pull altogether, of about 100 hands, we landed it safely on the hill, in the presence of a large number of enthusiastic onlookers.

(A locomotive nicknamed *Coppernob* because of its polished casing was for many years exhibited on the station at Barrow-in-Furness.)

The Furness was conceived as a goods line but for a time took passengers, though only on Sundays, quartering them in a sheep van that was 'fitted by a carpenter with neat deal seats'. Day-trippers arriving by sea were conveyed by rail to visit Furness Abbey, which now had its own station. Over time the Furness Railway absorbed other lines. In 1846 powers to extend the system east, from Barrow to Ulverston, were obtained, but the work was slow to develop. Ulverston was reached in 1854. The Furness directors jibbed at extending further east, and especially at the thought of building viaducts over the Leven and Kent estuaries. The link between Furness and the West Coast route was thus achieved through an independent promotion, the company concerned being the Ulverstone and Lancaster Railway. The Furness kept close ties through James Ramsden, who was appointed secretary. The outlay on the stretch of line that completed the coastal chain was an imposing £420,000, much of it expended on the viaducts. These were devised by James Brunlees of Manchester, who had experience in bridging and embanking marshy ground. In spanning the estuaries, he earned wide renown.

The initial probing of the estuaries was disappointing. Although boring operations extended to a depth of 90 feet, sand only was found. At Kent and Leven, Brunless skilfully used water jets to drive piles operating within immense, hollow, cast-iron

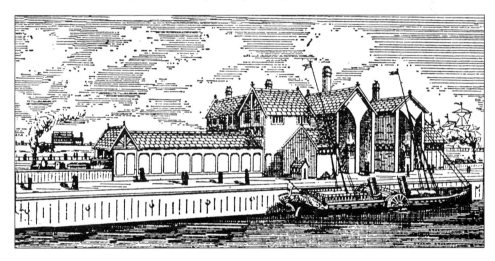

44   *Ramsden Dock station at Barrow-in-Furness.*

45   *For the railway viaduct over the Kent iron piers were sunk deep into the estuary.*

46   *Arnside station staff during the latter days of steam traction.*

columns. The Kent viaduct, with 30 50-ft bays, had a novel central feature: a telescopic shipping bay, which enabled vessels to pass up to Milnthorpe, though it was rarely used for this purpose. Around 1915, when the railway was handling heavy armaments from Barrow, the slender iron piers were filled up with concrete, encased in blue brick and eventually faced with stones.

Goods were being moved on the line from 10 August 1857, the opening having been twice delayed when ships collided with the Leven viaduct. Passenger traffic was operating from 26 August. A station initially named Cark-in-Cartmel (later Cark and Cartmel) served Holker Hall, a residence of the Duke of Devonshire who, having allowed the line to be built over part of his estate, expected express trains to acknowledge local passengers. Cark, with its ducal connections, was provided with an iron footbridge, a waiting room for important people, and platform seats with cast-iron bench-ends that featured a squirrel eating nuts. J.C. Dickinson relates that, with the arrival of rail travel, passenger traffic across Leven Sands slumped to a small number of folk, mostly tramps who could not afford the train fare. The guide, who was legally obliged to conduct people across the estuary, handed over the rail fare to one or two tramps to spare himself the trouble of guiding them. News of this largesse quickly spread. After tramps became numerous, the guide bought a horse. When the next tramp arrived, he said, 'I ride, you walk,' and the tramping fraternity had lost a source of easy money. The connection with the main line that transformed the village of Carnforth into a busy junction town was opened in September 1857, and absorbed by the Furness Railway in 1862.

Among the company's rural lines was one to Coniston, with a connecting steamer service on Coniston Water. Another, to Lakeside, connected with the Windermere steamers; the main revenue came from supplying them with coal, delivering iron ore to the Backbarrow ironworks and carrying the sulphur and saltpetre needed by the

Black Beck and Low Wood gunpowder works. In the other direction the system moved pig-iron, gunpowder, pit props, bobbins and 'dolly blue'. A branch of the Furness from Arnside to Hincaster Junction, established in 1876, was intended to speed up the delivery of coke from County Durham to the greedy ironworks of Furness. A service from Grange to Kendal used a locomotive nicknamed *Kendal Tommy*. At the century's end, small, six-wheeled slip-coaches were coupled to the rear of some trains bound for Ulverston at Carnforth. The coaches, intended for passengers to Grange, were uncoupled by the guard as the train neared Holme Island and came to rest at the station, so the main part of the train would not need to stop here. Next morning the slip-coaches were put on the up-line and returned to Carnforth.

Arthur Ransome, author of *Swallows and Amazons* and a host of other readable books about children in a Lakeland setting, knew the railway station at Greenodd from boyhood. His family lived in Leeds and holidays were spent at Nibthwaite, near the outflow of Coniston Water. During the train journey to Greenodd, Arthur looked out for well-known landmarks such as Arnside Tower, and, of course, views of the Kent estuary and Morecambe Bay. At Greenodd a Swainson from Nibthwaite, complete with horse and red farm cart, was ready to take them to their holiday haunt at a trot. At the end of one holiday young Arthur packed into a cardboard box all the creatures he had collected. As the Ransomes crossed the railway line, with the train from Lakeside in sight, Arthur slipped and fell. The box opened and his 'menagerie' was scattered in the path of the approaching train. The lad gave an anguished cry and began to pick up his living treasures. The stationmaster, who had reversed the signals and held

47   *Lakeside, Windermere, a railway terminus.*

48 *Captain Hamill and a model of the steamboat* Gondola, *which operated on Coniston Water.*

up the train on the bridge a few yards away, joined him. Together they rounded up a host of newts, caterpillars and other squirming creatures.

The success of the Furness Railway inhibited the development of the road system around Morecambe Bay. The main road was left virtually as the turnpike trustees had visualised it and was thus, in the 20th century, unprepared for the age of the motor car. What might have been done in the inter-war years to improve matters was evident from the construction of the Coast Road from Barrow to Ulverston by unemployed workers in the 1920s. The rail system declined from the late 1950s, when the Coniston branch created by the Furness Railway was closed to passengers; it was shut down in 1962. Passenger trains to Lakeside that had been operating only during the summer months were withdrawn in 1965. The branch closed in 1967, but its northern end began to operate again in 1973 under the auspices of the Lakeside and Haverthwaite Railway Company, who showed verve and imagination in its development. The main line remains busy.

Six

LANCASTER AND THE LUNE

From a fort built on a hill above the Lune, six miles from the open sea, a Roman garrison kept an eye on the point where, at low tide, the Lune was fordable and, at high water, was navigable. Shipping on the Lune would by the 18th century become the source of Lancaster's wealth. Meanwhile the river created problems. Not until the latter part of the 18th century would this tidal reach of the Lune be satisfactorily spanned. The imposing Skerton Bridge replaced a narrow old bridge across which horse-drawn coaches had clattered on their way to Hest Bank and the oversands route to Furness. Soon an aqueduct designed by John Rennie was carrying canal barges across the river. By the dawning of the railway age, the task of bridging the Lune was just another job. The original bridge for the Lancaster-Carlisle Railway had stone arches and timber spans. The stonework has endured, but the timber was replaced in the 1960s by steel and concrete.

In Norman times, Roger of Poitou had administered his vast estates, which extended from Furness to the Mersey, from quarters on the hill above the Lune where the Priory Church at Lancaster now stands. On the menu at that time was Lune salmon. The great fish and their cousins, the sea trout, were intercepted while on their spawning run to the gravel beds at the head of the valley. In 1180 Hugh Garth, 'a hermit of great perfection', came to Cockersands at the mouth of the Lune and was granted the Lune fishery. The monks of Cockersands Abbey, St Mary-of-the-Marsh, constructed a massive balk (a hedge of wattles standing on a bank of stone) near what is now the abbey light. The high tide covered it and fish were intercepted on the ebb. When Bishop Redman planned a visit he ordered that an experienced man should meet him at Lancaster so that he might be conducted safely 'amid all the dangers of the sea' to the abbey.

At the Dissolution Cockersands was accounted the third richest religious house in Lancashire, with an estimated income of £282 a year. Little of the abbey remains. The 14th-century choir stalls were moved to the parish church of Lancaster and the Daltons preserved the chapter house as a family vault. Some of the monastic sandstone was used to improve sea defences. Traces of it are also found in local buildings and some at Overton, across the Lune, a village that clung to a 50-ft hill, around which, until land was reclaimed in the 17th century, the tides raced. Following the abrupt ending of the abbey's life at the whim of Henry VIII, the rector of Cockerham had the right to remove salmon from the balk at certain tides, which became known as Parson's Tides.

49 *An old print of Lancaster Castle station in the 1840s.*

50 *View of Lancaster as it was in 1780.*

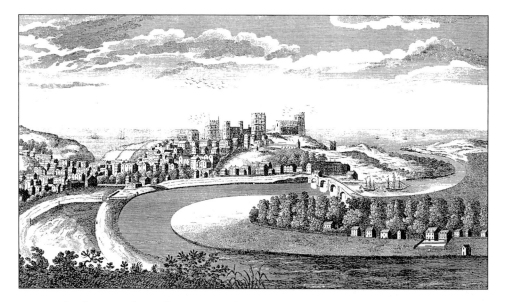

On the first two days of one September week in 1826, over 1,300 lb of fine salmon were caught by Mr R.F. Bradshaw's Halton fishery. In the first four days of July, seven years later, 439 salmon and 2,529 lb of smaller fish were taken in the Skerton fishery. Four hundred pounds of salmon were lifted from Skerton weirs on 13 September 1835. Seven years later, at the same fishery, the catch of salmon totalled 3,300 lb. On 29 July 1843, the *Gazette* reported that 'an enormous quantity of salmon has this week been taken at Skerton – on Monday, 98 fish weighing 1,142 lb; on Tuesday between 800 and 900 lb weight; and on Wednesday about 500 lb.' There were especially low prices because so many fish were being taken. The *Lancaster Gazette* recorded the landing of immense numbers of salmon in the early 1900s.

A westerly breeze, sweeping up the Lune from Morecambe Bay, rustles the leaves of trees planted on St George's Quay. Once a tumult of shipping activity, the area is now, under the auspices of Lancaster Corporation, a broad promenade. Elegant 18th-century warehouses (mainly converted into flats), slipways and mooring stones

evoke Lancaster's maritime glory days. Ships from the Lune traded around the Irish
Sea. By the 18th century local merchants had profitable links with the Baltic and the
West Indies. Robert Lawson, born in 1690, flourished in the shipping trade and in the
period from 1715 to 1720 developed the facilities at Sunderland Point, near the mouth
of the Lune, to the extent that ships might be built and fitted out here. He made
money through a variety of maritime enterprises, such as providing war transport
to Ireland during the campaign of William III. The merchant eventually over-reached
himself, however, and in 1729 was bankrupt, with debts amounting to about £14,000,
which he settled at the rate of only 14s. in the pound.

In 1749 a Port Commission came into being at Lancaster, with the aim of improving
the river channel and creating a stone quay, the cost being met by tolls. A splendid
Customs House, designed by Richard Gillow (more widely known as a maker of fine
furniture), was finished in 1764. Between 1750 and 1800 Lancaster merchants dealt in

51 *Lancaster Castle, a
prime vantage point for
Morecambe Bay.*

52 *Cockersands Abbey
on the flat land where
the Lune met the Bay.*

53   *A boatyard at the village of Overton, beside the Lune.*

the products of the West Indies: tobacco, sugar, rum, cotton, spices and mahogany. Lancaster exports boosted that trade and the town entered the trade in black slaves, though not as a major player. Lancaster became a stylish place with fine buildings in the 18th century, but Britain's fourth busiest port was beset by navigational problems on the Lune. A rock bar below St George's Quay limited the size of ships and an outpost was needed.

The idea of developing Sunderland Point was considered, but rejected because of its exposed position and tidal approach road. In 1779 the Port Commissioners focused on two farms, Glasson and Saltcote, knowing that ships had been moored off Glasson since 1751. The land was purchased from the Dalton family of Thurnam Hall. In a flurry of activity over eight years, a dock, with an attendant village, was conceived and created. By 1826 it also had canal facilities. With Glasson Dock operating five miles down the river from Lancaster, St George's Quay, once bustling with people and stacked high with bales and barrels, became a relatively quiet place. The decline of Lancaster as a port, partly due to the Napoleonic Wars, was mainly caused by the lusty growth of Liverpool in the 19th century. In turn, Glasson Dock had a powerful competitor from 1904, when the Midland Railway opened a handy new harbour at Heysham.

With its squares and narrow streets, its grandiose public buildings and wealth of 18th-century architecture, central Lancaster retains an old-time flavour. The oldest remaining house, known as the Judges' Lodgings, stands in an area where Romans once trod. The present building dates from about 1620. It was a private house until 1826, when it was adapted for the use of visiting judges at the Lancaster Assizes.

54 *Sunderland Point, at the mouth of the Lune, c.1960.*

55 *Victorian print of Sunderland Point. High tides cover the approach road.*

56 *Jim Braid, an Overton fisherman,*
operated one of the wammel *boats.*

57 *Salmon fishing on the River Lune.*

The imposing John o'Gaunt's Gateway gives access to Lancaster Castle, which is now an airy prison with reminders, in an area of public access, of times when the prisoners included Quakers and Pendle Witches. The old town hall in Market Square is now a museum. The present town hall, opened in 1909, was designed on a grand scale. A statue of Queen Victoria, centrepiece of a mini-park, maintains an unblinking stare at this seat of local government. Situated in Williamson Park, and the highest point in the city, is the Ashton Memorial, gleaming white and curiously oriental in style. Built in 1909, it reminds us of the Williamson family of floor-covering fame. It provides a prime viewpoint for Morecambe Bay.

Across the Lune, the approach to Sunderland Point from Overton is chancy, being subject to tides twice a day. Most of the families in Overton were once in farming or fishing. Worshippers attended St Helen's Church, an ancient foundation by the estuary, where there was a ferry connection with Glasson. The village pond was filled in and Overton School, which once had over 60 names on its register, has since become a private house. Fewer houses are now whitewashed, a custom which was once general. Walk around the streets and you see dated doorheads and the mullioned windows that connect properties with the closing years of the 17th century. It was about this time that the Woodhouse family set up a joinery business, their products including coffins. In due course they were also boat-builders, specialising in *wammels*, the small sailing craft used for salmon-netting in the Lune. The largest boat to leave the yard was a 21-ton yawl built for Arthur Mansergh in 1920. The last new boat to be made in the yard took form in the Second World War.

58 Haaf-net *fishing by the Lune. This hand-held net is of Norse design.*

59 A wammel *under sail on the Lune.*

Sunderland Point was, for a time, a reception area for the treasures of the Indies. It is claimed that the first cotton to reach England was dumped here and remained unattended for a year until someone discovered a way of using it. The so-called 'cotton tree', which blossoms each summer, developed from a seed that was not of the ordinary cotton shrub, but a kapok tree of the species *Bonbax pentandrum*. It occurs in the Indies.

At both Overton and Sunderland Point were small wooden huts where fishermen kept their tackle. Working garb comprised ganseys, corduroy trousers and rubber waders. For two months of the year the Lunebank communities intercepted salmon (*Salmo salar*) and sea trout (*Salmo trutta*) using nets paid out from small boats or (while wading chest deep) with the *haaf-net*, a cumbersome device consisting of a long wooden frame and two purse nets. The haaf-net, held against the ebb in a tidal river, is said to derive its name from the Norse word for sea. Dr F.W. Hogarth, of Morecambe, who studied the Viking period, believed that the curious duplication of the vowel sound in local words denoted a Norse origin. Other examples include *skeer*, a patch of rough seabed left dry by an ebb tide, *roost*, a tidal rip or drop-off, *craam*, an iron rake with a wooden shaft used for gathering up bunches of cockles, and *laaster*, a three-pronged spear used to impale fish in shallow water or to capture salmon on their spawning run.

60 *Landing a catch of fish from the Lune.*

61 *Cock salmon from the River Lune. The fish has a hooked lower jaw.*

The Lune was never taken for granted. A bore swept up the estuary with the incoming tide and, below Sunderland Point, the river had been known to change its course by half a mile in 12 months. A sailing boat which had foundered, losing its crew, illustrates this: one year the river ran beside the wreck; the following year the wreck lay half a mile from the river's course.

Far up the Lune, farm lads 'put a set or two of click-hooks in their pockets and went down t'becks looking in t'dubs. If they saw salmon, they cast their lines and lait 'em out'. In the 1930s and 1940s poaching salmon was a means of providing 'fill-belly' for people faring badly in straitened times. Spare fish were given away. The poachers operated at all times, noon and night, 'as long as nobody was watching and t'fish didn't go away'. But chiefly it was at night, with a light, that poaching took place. If a bailiff or a policeman drafted in during the peak of the poaching season arrived, he might hear a flute-like whistling. It was not made by an otter, but by a poacher warning his friends of an intruder. A poacher carried a cobble the size of a duck egg and, when necessary, tossed it into a pool as a warning. Back home the salmon steaks might be rolled in oatmeal and fried for dinner.

When the author first knew the Lune, fishermen operating from Sunderland Point and Glasson Dock were rivals at wammeling. Jim Braid, of Overton, described the drift-net used as comprising 320 yards of material. It was paid out from the stern of a 20-ft clinker-built

62 *Lune salmon fishermen. Fish in the upper reaches were sometimes poached.*

63 *Cotton tree at Sunderland Point, which was a reception area for the treasures of the Indies.*

64 *Cotton Tree Cottage, Sunderland Point.*

boat, which was initially under lug-sail but was subsequently powered by an engine. The original boats were hard to operate because of the transom stern. The best type of boat, according to Jim, was one that did not draw much water, for, after all, a salmon worked the shallows. With the right sort of current, the fisherman had to get out the oars. In sailing conditions the white sails took on a ruddy hue, having been dipped in preservatives. It was, said Jim, a case of 'red sails in the sunset'.

An engine was used for getting to 'somewhere' to shoot the net. 'The force of water spread the net, so we liked a good breeze.' A fisherman would set off at about three hours' ebb, get his net out, drift down, then use the sail to move across the river or return to shoot again. Jim Braid, dissatisfied with the type of boat he first used, ordered another from the yard of Mr Goodall, at Sandsend near Whitby. The boat was built to a local design: 'They fetched it here. Next thing, everybody was wanting a boat like it.' Jim's sons took a mould and made 16 replicas in fibreglass. When Jim installed an engine in his boat other local fishermen thought it was wrong, yet 'if conditions were quiet, they were keen enough to take their anchor in and let me tow them'.

At the time Jim Braid was working the Lune he encountered a large number of big sea trout – five to seven pounders – from the middle of May until June: 'They cut as pink as salmon.' One Lune drift-netter caught a bottle-nosed dolphin by the mouth. He realised that something was amiss when nearly thirty of the 175 corks that gave the net buoyancy went under water. Still concerned at the rate at which his netting rotted, Jim bought some green preservative – the sort used for garden fencing – and without letting anyone know of his intentions he sunk a third of a net into a tub of the liquid. The other fishermen were soon aware that that this piece of net was lasting longer than theirs; it was good for 28 weeks. Said Jim:

> I went out with a man on a day when the water was so clear you could see crabs
> and shrimps moving about. That green bit o' net was close to the boat. The man

65 *The grave of Sambo, a negro houseboy, at Sunderland Point (see page 39).*

66 *Trawlers at Glasson Dock, five miles downriver from Lancaster.*

67   *Salmon hatchery in the Lune Valley.*

said, 'Eey, look – there's a salmon.' It was coming alongside the white net towards us. As soon as it got to t'green net, it was caught. It wasn't long before another salmon had done the same.

The other fishermen were soon asking Jim the source of his 'green stuff'.

A draw net, now only a remote memory, was paid out from a boat moving in a broad semi-circle. Two groups of men were needed, one where the net entered the water and another group near the land which was ready to scramble ashore to control it. Then the two ends were pulled, and any luckless fish that had been in the area came up along with the net.

Haaf-nets belonging to some of the fishermen dried out when propped against walls at the *Golden Ball*, between Lancaster and Overton. (This hostelry was known locally as 'Snatchem's', supposedly from the days when the Navy relied on the press-gang to augment its crews.) When operating the haaf (pronounced 'hayve'), a fisherman stood facing the current. The net billowed out behind in two large pockets or bags. A captured salmon was despatched by a smart tap on the head with a stick resembling a truncheon. A haaf-netter told Herbert C. Collins about his method of fishing. He used to plant his net in front of a deep hole in the river bed. Here he would stand for eight hours a day from May until the end of August, with only a break for meals. The odds against a catch were great:

> Sometimes they're moving tail forrard and when they feel t'net they spring away. At night phosphorus on t'net keeps 'em away. It's best after a shower of rain. Then t'fish move downriver afore t'flood watter or if they're still in't channel t'rain watter from streets o' Lancaster pour its muck in't river an' t'fish can't see so weel so they bump into net.

In the quest for fish, the Braids sailed as far down the coast as Hilbre Island, in Liverpool Bay. Jim lost a boat off Fleetwood when he was knocked overboard at night and the boat kept moving. 'In those days we had double-skin overalls, with a belt. My life was saved by a pocket of air.' Jim and his son David usually operated to the point where the Lune merged with the open Bay, where there were other rivers making their presence felt.

> When three currents are working out there, it can make a mess of things. We'd run down to the Lune Deeps but couldn't get through that area when the waves were mountains high. The worst conditions were at five to six hours' ebb, when it's running the hardest. I'm talking about big tides – those coming up the banks!

Seven

HEYSHAM AND MORECAMBE

Heysham

Today, although apparently swamped by Morecambe, Heysham remains a proud place which is distinguished in the Morecambe Bay area by being sheltered by a headland composed of millstone grit. Holidaymakers come here to splash and paddle. A natural rock arch has long been known as the Fairy Chapel. Heysham's early population was small enough for everyone to be on first-name terms; like other local communities, they farmed and fished. As an old rhyme had it, 'Heysham for size and Middleton for grips, Overton for dancing schools and Sunderland for ships.' In the redistribution of land after the Conquest, Roger de Poitou was given Lower Heysham and its two churches, which he granted to the Abbey of St Martin, Sees. In the early medieval period the lord of Upper Heysham was bound, if the king came to Lancashire, to welcome him with horn and white staff at the county boundary. He also had to be on hand when the monarch departed.

68 *Engraving of Heysham, an old village sheltered by a gritstone headland.*

69   *Bare, a village that was absorbed into the resort of Morecambe.*

One of the churches is still in use; the other is a dignified skyline ruin. Both date back to the Dark Ages. St Peter's Church looks ancient, as well it might, having a modicum of masonry that was put in place before the Norman Conquest. The building seen today is a consequence of rebuilding and enlargement to meet changing needs. Carvings on a hogsback tombstone in the south aisle testify to an ancient past and hint at the change from Norse paganism to Christian witness. St Patrick's Chapel, high lying with sweeping views of Morecambe Bay, pre-dates the saint who became its patron. There remain an arched doorway, low walls and eight graves cut into a rock outcrop, with sockets in which wooden crosses would be placed. They are not unlike the rock-hewn graves found at Hexham, in Old Northumbria, and in Ireland. Originally a stone lid would have sealed each grave. Interments were still taking place on the south side of the chapel in the 10th and 11th centuries.

For centuries Heysham folk lived mainly by tending the land, which was under pasture, and fishing. They also gathered mussels on the skears, transporting them to the shore by horse-drawn cart. Heysham Head, now owned by the National Trust, is a conspicuous feature on what is mainly a low-lying coastline, seen at its best from the romantically named Half Moon Bay. The village, keen to attract visitors, was proud of its ornamental gardens – and its nettle beer. For many years it remained a quiet, picturesque little place. Then, early in the 20th century, there was disturbance on a massive scale. The Midland Railway Company, which had not long completed its Settle-Carlisle railway, which had provided a direct link with Scotland, turned its attention to Ireland. Morecambe had a tidal harbour based on the stone jetty, but this was restricted by shallow water. The Midland proposed to make a deep water harbour for

70   *Heysham, an ancient village mentioned in Domesday Book.*

passengers and goods at Heysham. Work on the project began in 1897. The Cawthra family, taking fright, sold Heysham Tower to the Midland as a hotel. Light aircraft, which had landed on a sandy beach at Middleton in the absence of a local airfield, were no longer able to do this.

An imaginative scheme was devised for Heysham Harbour. Two huge breakwaters, linked by a temporary dam, extended the promontories of Red Nab and Near Naze towards a submarine valley lying offshore. Part of the reclaimed area would be transformed into a new port by dredging a channel into deep water. The harbour, entirely artificial and tailor-made for the railway custom, was the first port in Britain to be operated entirely by electricity. The enterprise cost the Midland £3m and sent a few shivers through the ranks of the shareholders. After its completion, the last sailing from Morecambe Harbour to Dublin took place on 31 August 1904. On

71   *St Peter's Church, Heysham, the oldest part of which pre-dates the Norman Conquest.*

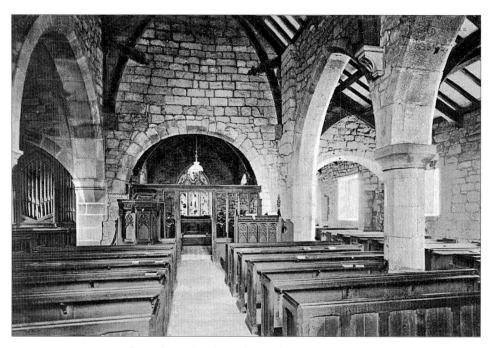

72   *Interior of Heysham Church. In the south aisle is a hogsback tombstone.*

73   *Ruins of St Patrick's, Heysham. The chapel is older than its present name implies.*

74 *Stone graves, Heysham. When used, inscribed stones would cover them.*

the following day Heysham Harbour opened for trade. A service to Belfast was added to that for Dublin.

The proprietors of the Heysham-Belfast ferry service, exploiting Lancaster's position on the London to Glasgow railway line, laid a branch line through Green Ayre and Morecambe to the new harbour. Rail passengers could thus disembark within a few paces of the ferry. The sea link with Ireland operated from 1905 until 1975 when, owing to declining demand, it came to an end, leaving just one ferry to serve the Isle of Man. In its early days Heysham Harbour received boats with imported raw materials – timber from Sweden or cork for Williamson's linoleum works in Lancaster. Heysham went into the oil business with an ocean jetty, built from north breakwater to the edge of what had become known as Heysham Lake. Laden tankers could thus discharge their cargoes for a new refinery that stood less than two miles away. The blocky grey form of the Heysham atomic power station is now visible from virtually every viewpoint along the shores of the Bay.

Morecambe

One must grant the resort of Morecambe a superb situation. Dias Cromerty, in *Picturesque Lancashire*, found Morecambe very 'shoppy' and the promenade 'staring', with 'Amusements' written loud and large all over it. Yet even the most exacting of critics will own that Morecambe has spectacular sunsets, 'with the sun going down splendidly beyond the Irish Sea. All Lakeland, to the north, catches the glow.' The resort dates from the middle of the 19th century, when rail links with the industrialised

75   *The wharf, when Morecambe still had a busy harbour.*

towns of Yorkshire and Lancashire led to a boom in seaside holidays. Morecambe was grafted on to several small hamlets, including Poulton, Bare and Torrisholme.

Thomas Gray, a visitor to the district in 1772, had found himself in a fishing village called Poulton-le-Sands, where old houses were surrounded on three sides by fields and a 'chappell' served the community's spiritual needs. Gray saw a few fishermen repairing nets on a shingle beach. He was told by them that one foggy day a father, mother and two daughters had been trudging home from from the low-tide fishing grounds with their horse when the man, seeking a safe way across the channels, was drowned. His wife drowned while looking for him. The girls, following the horse, reached the sanctuary of the shore.

A hint of the future role for this area came with the popularity of sea bathing from the 1820s, although the resident population of what was still known as Poulton-le-Sands was fewer than four hundred. A regatta featuring rowing matches, held on 24 July 1829, was interrupted by a thunderstorm. In the following year, at what had been abridged to Poulton, the fishermen had a second chance to demonstrate their sailing prowess. People heading for the event could use a coach, the *Old Times*, that ran from Lancaster. A steamer called *Windermere* berthed at Morecambe to collect tourists for the Lake District. When a third regatta was held, on 22 July 1831, the name of the up-and-coming bayside resort had changed from Poulton to Morecambe. The arrival of the railway in 1847 stimulated tourism and opened up the markets of the West Riding and Lancashire to the products of the Bay, especially cockles. A steamer service between Morecambe and Belfast began in 1847 and continued for some twenty years before being transferred to Barrow. Morecambe's first pier, extending 912 feet into the bay, was opened in March 1869 and, from a landing stage at the end, people boarded steamers for Ireland. The owners of smaller craft offered trips round the Bay.

The aforementioned branch line between Lancaster (Green Ayre) and Morecambe seafront having opened in 1848, a wooden jetty was available for shipping. An increase in traffic led to the making of a stone pier in 1853. It was much longer than the wooden jetty and close enough to it for what was in effect a small harbour to be created.

With indifferent weather, holidaymakers craved an indoor centre. A major place of entertainment for visitors opened in 1874, and was grandly known as 'Morecambe

76   West End Pier, Morecambe, a resort that evolved from a fishing village called Poulton.

77   Landing stage, Morecambe, once much favoured by the citizens of Bradford.

78   *Morecambe in 1925. The name was adopted in 1889.*

79   *The Clock Tower, Morecambe, which dates from Edwardian days.*

Baths, Winter Palace and Aquarium', a name that was soon contracted to the Winter
Gardens. In 1889 the name Morecambe was adopted for the town. In a vigorous
building boom in which West Riding 'brass' was evident, the place was nicknamed
Bradford-by-the-Sea. The west end of the town soon reached the boundary with
Heysham and an Urban District came into being in 1894. (The town would receive
its Charter of Incorporation as a borough in 1902.)

Morecambe had its last fling as a marine centre with a ship-breaking yard run
from the stone jetty by T.W. Ward and Company, of Sheffield. The first vessel to
arrive, in September 1905, was a huge sailing ship called *Northampton*. The most
famous vessel, a White Star liner named SS *Majestic*, was broken up in 1914. Far
from being discouraged by the dust and noise, visitors to Morecambe queued and
paid for admission to obsolete liners and warships. The ship-breaking ended in 1934.
(The old wooden jetty was demolished in the mid-1950s but the stone pier remains.)
John Robert Birkett, who was Mayor from 1903 until 1906, donated the Clock Tower,
which gave flair to the seafront.

Style on a grander scale came in 1907 with the replacement of the railway station
by a structure with a frontage of 250 feet and a vast 'circulating area', a style described
as Elizabethan Gothic. Across the road was the *North Western Hotel*, originally built
in 1847, and subsequently named the *Midland Hotel*. This was in turn replaced, in

80   *Morecambe Harbour in 1931, when it was used for ship-breaking.*

1933, by the *New Midland*, a structure with a daring contemporary style. In October 1926 the last horse-drawn tram was hauled into history by the oldest available horses, aptly named Adam and Eve. There were few regrets, for Morecambe had already introduced the country's first petrol tram, which had its first run in 1912. During the First World War it would be run on town gas.

Morecambe's popularity as a holiday resort increased steadily until the 1970s, when a combination of mediocre weather and the arrival of cheap package holidays in sunnier climes led to a fall in visitor numbers. The fishing activity had also declined, and by the 1980s fewer than a dozen fishing boats were in regular use. Taking the place of the graceful nobbies were fibreglass boats with a much wider beam. They were known scathingly at Morecambe as 'plastic boats'. The 'TERN' project was developed to regenerate the town's tourist aspect, and special attention was given to the seafront.

The shore might lack extensive natural deposits of sand for children to play in, but the town's setting to the south of Morecambe Bay offers a view of the ever-changing Bay and the Lakeland fells. On clear evenings there are sunsets that vie with those of the Hebrides. The developed seafront is now over five miles long, with new defences against the cruel sea. A statue of Eric Morecambe, the comedian, in his distinctive one-legged pose, was unveiled here by the Queen. The Bay's outstanding bird life is reflected in features on the new coastal defences and promenade. Roundabouts on the new Central Drive are festooned with steel cormorants, gannets and razorbills. Cast-iron cormorants perch on bollards. Flocks of metal birds create the illusion that they are in wheeling flight. There are, of course, real-life seagulls galore.

Eight

ARNSIDE AND SILVERDALE

J.A. Steers, of St Catherine's College, Cambridge, in his book *The Coast Line of England and Wales*, considered that the finest coastal scenery on Morecambe Bay is near Silverdale and Arnside. Hereabouts, woodland and small valleys, and the marshes running up to the high ground, form an unusual picture. 'As in all places where there are extensive sands exposed at low water, the tides in their changing cycles add enormously to the beauty of the landscape and this is especially true in these mountain-enclosed estuaries.' The villages of Arnside and Silverdale stand on a peninsula washed by the rivers Keer and Kent. What remains of the limestone scenery after centuries of quarrying is being conserved within an Area of Outstanding Natural Beauty. At Gait Barrows, a nature reserve of 180 acres purchased to mark the Queen's Silver Jubilee in 1977, the bared bones of a classic limestone landscape have been scoured by glacial action and eroded by rain that contains a weak solution of acid. The result is a spectacular expanse of 'pavements', which was composed of blocks of stone known as 'clints', each separated from its neighbours by fissures called 'grykes' and drainage channels known as 'runnels'. Alien boulders, first borne and then dumped by a melting ice-sheet, are known as 'erratics'.

With abundant rain, the soil has acquired a sweetness that appeals to over 400 species of plant on a 200-acre tract. The grykes shelter them from the worst of the weather. In times past they had to contend with attention from hungry sheep. Some species of tree found here are at the northern limit of their range. Examples include the wild service tree and the small-leaved lime. The latter, which is locally prominent, is a useful indicator of primary woodland. Beech growing hereabouts has especially white timber. In the deciduous woodland of the peninsula live free-ranging red, roe and fallow deer; in the glades on Arnside Knott, a well wooded hill with an elevation of 522 feet, the Scots Argus butterfly is found, known elsewhere in England only in Smardale, Edenvale.

Arnside and Silverdale were home to a few farmers and fishermen. At small quarries, limestone was lifted for building or, burnt in field kilns, was spread on the land to sweeten it. Arnside is compact and Silverdale widely spread.

Arnside

For the pre-Victorian churchgoers of Arnside there was a Sunday walk by rough track and across two scars to the church at Beetham. The first scar was easily negotiated;

81   *Kent estuary from Arnside. A flow tide is preceded by a bore, or wall of water.*

a natural rising cleft on the second scar had steps cut into it. They are known as the Fairy Steps. Arnside's nautical air originates in the proverbial mists of time, and we know that Henry VIII charged one of the Clifford family, as Admiral, with the safety of the coast. Clifford must have had men and ships available in an emergency. The *Directory* of 1849 stated that Arnside Sands 'are covered one hour with ships and another with carriages and pedestrians'.

Arnside had a salt industry until the closing years of the 18th century, when Warrington and Cheshire took most of the trade. At Saltcotes, built in 1679, two windows were knocked into one when the infamous Window Tax was introduced in 1695 to provide a guaranteed income for the newly established Bank of England.

Arnside Tower was one of several peles where the populace could find sanctuary when Scottish pirates were on the rampage. A pele, with ultra-thick walls and crenallation, had accommodation for people and stock. Examples were to be found at Dalton, on Piel Island and, to the east of the Bay, at Arnside, Hazelslack, Beetham, Dallam and Levens. Peles at Dallam and Levens were to form the core of stately homes.

At Arnside, where the sound of a buzzer warned people of the impending arrival of the tide, the bore continued to fascinate both visitors and natives. Desmond Burrow, whom the author met at his home overlooking the sparkling Kent estuary, said, 'If it's a spring tide, some ten minutes later you'll see the bore appear, roaring by, with water that extends right up to the promenade.' In a strange way, the railway viaduct enhances the estuary. This triumph of engineering has 50 arches, and though its feet are buried in sand it stands firm against the boisterous winds, river and the encroaching tides. It has been known for spume from angry waves to shower passing trains. The viaduct is popularly said to be as long in yards (520) as Arnside Knott is high in feet. Surveys determined that the best way across the estuary was an old ford. An unexpected bonus, when the viaduct had taken shape, was the reclamation of a large tract of land. The railway company claimed it and their case was upheld in court. The lord of the manor, miffed, took the matter as far as the Exchequer, but had to be content with around four hundred acres.

A wide promenade, dating from Jubilee year (1897), was ideal for strolling; it was also popular with artists. By 1914 the population of Arnside was rather more than a thousand and the village had acquired a row of private houses and a shop, all with a clear view of the estuary. *The Albion Hotel* was built in 1821 for Robert Bush, master mariner. In Edwardian days it was run by William James Bush. A jetty in stone replaced one of wood in a scheme devised by the Ulverstone and

Lancaster Railway Company. It was needed after the construction of the Kent railway viaduct caused the estuary to silt up, limiting the size of ships sailing to the port of Milnthorpe. The stone jetty provided a wharf for seaborne traffic. Storm-wracked on several occasions, and purchased from the LMS Railway Company for £100, the jetty is now in good condition.

Crossfield Brothers, the builders of Morecambe trawlers, earned Arnside renown for the quality of their work. The firm began as joiners and cabinet-makers. Richard Burrow, the last full-time fisherman at Arnside, had a boat called *Girl Pat*. She was a heavy boat, built for safety purposes. He paid £5 for it and made it available to sea-anglers. His son, Desmond, related that one day his father took half a dozen anglers and their tackle on board, along with six crates of beer. *Girl Pat* was towed out into the Bay. By lunchtime of that glorious summer's day, all that could be seen were six pairs of feet extending over the gunwales, accompanying six rods protruding from the boat: 'The men had drunk enough beer to make them sleepy.' Upon their return to shore, they bought some fluke from Mr Burrow and took them home to impress their wives.

Silverdale

The Ballad of Flodden Field includes the couplet, 'From Silverdale to Kent sand side, Whose soil is sown with cockle shells'. Silverdale (so named since about 1500) is a sprawling village with no real centre, chiefly consisting of a smattering of farms and a quarry that in its heyday employed most of the local men. Above a silted-up cove is an oratory built as a personal chapel for Henry Boddington. The railway station is not conveniently situated, being three-quarters of a mile from the village at its nearest point.

A chimney of 18th-century origin is a prominent feature of the shore at Jenny Brown's Point. The chimney testifies to the presence of a copper-smelting mill built by Welshmen. It is said that Paddikan, the name of a large house on the shore, is derived from the Irish term for billets; Irishmen were among the workers in an ill-fated scheme to reclaim Silverdale Sands. A footpath leads to the Pepper Box, a name given to a Queen Victoria Golden Jubilee monument raised on Castlebarrow. In Regency times a bath-house stood among a row of cottages on Silverdale's shore, and bathing was noted here as recently as the 1860s. At one time it was common for doctors to recommend Silverdale as a health resort.

Silverdale has strong literary associations. Charlotte Brontë stayed here as a girl. She and her sisters were attending the Clergy Daughters' School at Cowan Bridge when there was an outbreak of low fever. The Rev. W. Carus Wilson, who had founded the school, owned Cove House at Silverdale, to which the Brontë lasses were moved to avoid infection. Elizabeth Gaskell, biographer of Charlotte, visited Gilbraltar Farm in 1850 and wrote of Silverdale that it could hardly be called the seaside: it was a little dale running down to Morecambe Bay. When, in 1858, the Gaskells paid a return visit to Gibraltar Farm, Elizabeth described their accommodation as 'a queer, pretty crampy house, at the back of a great farmhouse'. In the garden was 'an old Square Tower, or "Peel" – a remnant of the Border towers'. In truth, the tower had been built in the 19th century.

The poet Edward Thomas, visiting his friend Gordon Bottomley at Silverdale in 1916 (not long before his death on the Western Front), wrote of Bottomley's house, the 'Sheiling', 'It stands alone / Up in a land of stone / All worn like ancient stairs, / A land of rocks and trees / Nourished on wind and stone.' When a parcel for Bottomley arrived at Silverdale by train, the boy who delivered it would receive sixpence. Gordon emulated his father, who lived locally, in sporting a long beard.

82 *Jenny Brown's Point. The Chimney was built when copper was being smelted hereabouts.*

83   *The Cove, Silverdale, now silted, once received small coasting ships.*

William Riley, a Bradfordian who spent his 'sunset years' at Silverdale, wrote many books, one of which, *The Silver Dale*, was set in the area. The author remembers Riley as a kindly, old-fashioned man who, in his prime, as author of a novel called *Windyridge*, was a popular preacher in Methodist chapels over a wide area.

Leighton Moss, now a reserve of the Royal Society for the Protection of Birds, is an example of reclaimed land that was allowed to go back to nature. In 1848 Richard Thomas Gill reclaimed it from Morecambe Bay; he and his successors maintained it in good order by dint of pumping excess water into the Bay twice a day. Coal for the pump was transported from Silverdale station. Towards the end of the First World War, when the cost of pumping became prohibitive and fuel was in short supply, those concerned with the pump went to law. Meanwhile, the pump was stopped and the ground gradually returned to its old, sodden, reedy state. The face of Leighton Hall, built in the Gothic style of about 1800, is composed of white limestone, contrasting markedly with the greens of expansive parkland. The hall occupies the site of a fortified manor house of the 13th century. Sir George, last of the Middletons of Leighton, was a notable Cavalier. A colonel in the Royal Army, he was both knighted and made baronet at Durham on the same day in 1642. He was twice appointed High Sheriff of Lancaster.

84   *Gibraltar Farm, Silverdale, was visited by the novelist Elizabeth Gaskell.*

85   *Dallam Tower, Milnthorpe, home of the Wilson family.*

Kent Estuary

The river Kent, swiftest river in England, has its source in Kentmere, 1,000 feet above sea level. When prolonged rain falls around the headwaters, low water may become a full flood just 12 to 24 hours later, as the town of Kendal knows to its cost. Edwin Waugh was told that the Kent 'is seldom two days together in one place. You may make a chart one day and before the ink is dry it will have shifted.' A road from Arnside to Milnthorpe runs beside the estuary. Sandside, a small cluster of buildings, is bounded on one side by the Dixies and on the other by St John's Cross. Most of its marsh has been washed away by the tides. Anglers are spaced out along the promenade as they fish for fluke, using lines baited with red worms. The village of Storth, a Norse name meaning 'woody place', sits back from the shore.

Dykes reared beside Kent estuary held the restless tides at bay – most of the time. A disaster of 16 March 1907 passed into folklore and was even recounted in a novel, *The Lonely Plough*, written by Constance Holme, daughter of a land agent, and published in 1914. The characters in the novel enacted their lives against high wind and swirling water. The real flood occurred at around midnight one night when a gale arose, giving extra force to a high tide. When the tidal bore and south-west gale met a swollen river, the pressure burst the dykes near Foulshaw. At Low Foulshaw 22 sheep drowned, and at the farmhouse boots, pots, pans and peat turves were left floating in the kitchen. The flood licked the doorstep at High Foulshaw and 28 sheep perished. No human lives were lost. The central theme of Holme's novel is the ambition of a land agent to build an embankment and reclaim a valuable tract of land. The writer drew on the real-life story of the Brogden embankment, with which old Col Brogden hoped to restrain the tides. Afflicted by storm, the dyke was overrun. Constance Holme's novels evoke a former way of life in South Westmorland; she combined the topic of overriding interest with the concerns of the locality. We read (in *Beautiful End*) of the *boon-clip* (a sheep-shearing) at Appleton Hall. She showed that the austere life of farm folk and cottagers affected their outlook and often resulted in a fatalistic philosophy: what must be, must be.

Joe Cookson, a former headmaster at Milnthorpe, was another person with a deep feeling for the estuary of the Kent. He recalled that farms on Foulshaw, west of the estuary, were owned by Dallam Tower estate and farmed by entrenched local families such as the Ormerods and Bennetts. Most of the western side of Foulshaw was covered by peat that was, in some places, 15 feet deep. Two farms, Parsonage and Beetham Hall, standing on the eastern side of the estuary used peat as fuel. The peats were cut and dried on Foulshaw, then transported on horse-drawn carts using a low-tide route across Kent estuary. In due course the Land Commission transformed Foulshaw Farm and 1,600 acres of primeval bog into good pastureland. The area still attracts a wintering flock of about two hundred Icelandic greylags; they frequent these 'flats' and commute to quiet areas of the Lune Valley.

In the Kent estuary, herons from Dallam Tower stalk fish and eels at the confluence of Kent, Gilpin and Bela. In 1720, when the port of Milnthorpe was thriving, Daniel Wilson (1680-1754), who for 40 years was M.P. for Westmorland, set men to work rebuilding Dallam Tower, transforming it into a classic small country house, complete with a park inhabited by light-phase fallow deer. Just after the Second World War Sir Clement Jones toured Westmorland, 'that part of England were you can scramble or ramble or just amble', and of Dallam Tower he wrote that it has the perfect setting of an English country house. His assessment was based on its 'picked position', with the river in front and a hill behind, and on its parkland surroundings, all ringed round with a wall.

> You can see it from the Milnthorpe road. You can walk through the park, as my wife and I have done, over the hill to Storth. There are features at this place very like those at Rydal – the undulating park, the beck through it, the high ground and woods behind the house. I have sometimes thought that when the Wilsons of Dallam Tower and the Flemings of Rydal Hall inter-married, as they did more than once in the 18th century, each of them must have felt very much at home in the other's house.

One of our finest 16th-century houses, Levens Hall is regularly 'open to view'. In olden times the Mayor and Corporation of Kendal attended Milnthorpe Fair and, on their return home, stopped at Levens Hall to drink 'reddishes [a potent ale] and drink Morrocco [sic] till the sun went to bed'. The health of the owner of the Hall was toasted and he was wished all the luck he could desire 'while Kent flowed'. Visitors to the house learn that the house was planned in 1585 by Sir James Bellingham and that it has scarcely been altered since then. Col. Grahme, a Yorkshireman who bought the hall in 1690, took pity on Monsieur Beaumont, an out-of-work gardener who had served James II and designed the grounds of Hampton Court, and employed him to beautify the grounds. It was a task that lasted for years. The result of his efforts is a garden rich in topiary work. In Levens Park live a herd of dark-phase fallow deer and distinctive Bagot goats. They bear the surname of the family who have long since owned Levens Hall and its estate.

Road to Grange

Turnpike trustees built the road that runs westwards from Levens Bridge. Sampool Bridge spans the Gilpin, a river draining the north-south Lyth Valley which opens its mouth to mild breezes from Morecambe Bay. A limestone vale, sheltered on its sides by hill ranges, it is noted for the abundance and quality of its damsons. Damson trees are grouped together by the score or scattered along the hedgerows, although planting trees here has not been a good proposition; the hedges have suffered. Fifty years ago, James Edward Inman, of Draw Well Farm, had 700 damson trees on his land. After his father arrived at the farm, seven years elapsed without a single damson forming, yet the year before John Edward's tenancy there had been a crop of 16 tons. May is blossom time in the valley and damsons are usually ready for picking during the first week in September. During the Second World War people cycled from as far away as Preston and parts of Cheshire to buy half a stone of damsons at the farm. Years before, the crop had been carted to Kendal and sold at the street market. Mr Inman once took two cartloads of the fruit and disposed of it at sixpence a score, when its picking had cost threepence.

A stone tablet on Bowland Bridge marked the boundary between Crosthwaite and Lyth in Westmorland and Cartmel Fell in Lancashire. The local folk whitewash their

86 *Map of Leighton Moss.*

houses in spring, when the frosts have ended, and the sight is dazzling in a burst of spring sunshine. Here, half a century ago, Mrs Violet Parkinson was Sub-Postmistress and ran the village shop. The hamlet had half a dozen houses and a population of 10, three of them male. In her mother's day the shop had a large board for Lancashire cheese and barrels containing sugar. Tea was displayed in bulk and coffee was ground on the premises. Farm butter retailed at nine or ten pence a pound but in summer the price might drop to eight pence. In steady demand were cow bands, cart ropes, horse-halters and bacon strings.

The prominent white hill that is aptly known as Whitbarrow has outstanding examples of limestone pavement, with attendant plant life including dark-red helleborine and hoary rock rose. Butterfly species include high brown fritillary and pearl-bordered fritillary. Part of this prominent limestone hill, which rises above (and dominates) a section of the A590 near Witherslack, has been designated a National Nature Reserve. Involved in the care of the 570-acre reserve are the Lake District National Park Authority, the Forestry Commission and Cumbria Wildlife Trust. Healthy populations of juniper and ash woodland thrive here.

When a new stretch of road was built on the flats between Levens Bridge and a roundabout near Lindale, to improve the link with Barrow-in-Furness, a peculiar problem was faced. What should be done about the peat that had accumulated in those parts to a depth of some twenty feet? It was said that an old road across Foulshaw Mosses had been made using bundles of faggots. For the new super-highway it was not possible to remove all the peat, so stones were laid to compress it and after settlement a layer of reinforced concrete was added. The new road went on top. Meanwhile, life went on as usual on Whitbarrow Moss. Jim Wetton was among those with a right of *turbary*, allowed to cut peat for fuel, and recalled when peat

87   *John Wilson, for many years warden of the nature reserve on Leighton Moss.*

was used for the fire by blacksmiths putting metal hoops on the wheels of carts. Peat kept the home fires burning and at Low Levens the 'peat fireplace' had a capacity of 200 peats, which were also known as turves.

The inexpensive fuel was cut in May so that it might be dry and ready to take away by October. At the start of the operation a *tom spade* was used to remove the top material. Then a square-mouthed spade and a *peat spade* were brought into use. The latter measured 14 inches by five inches and had a single wing, known as a *cock*. A *sluff*, made of wood and with a metal tip to the blade, was ideal for cleaning out the dykes. At Witherslack Moss the peat was cut horizontally, unlike in other areas, where it was done vertically. The first layer of peat was called *fey*, beneath which lay *grey peat*, which was 'fuzzy'. Then came a layer of *black peat*, which was the best. The dark brown bottom-peats were known as *short metal*. This stuff would break up when wet and was 'no good for burning'. Below this was more greyish stuff. Then the peat-digger came to clay.

The peats were allowed to dry slowly, first being spread out on the ground. The next stage of the drying process, known as a *windrow*, saw two peats laid flat and two reared on edge above them, then two more laid flat on top, and so on, until the structure was six or seven peats deep. The traditional type of peat-barrow, with a small wheel and capacious back, had a capacity of 50 freshly cut peats or over 100 dried peats. For a time after drying, these were stored in a shed on the moss. The shed was made of wood and had a corrugated zinc roof. Jim Wetton said, 'The best way to stack peats in a shed is to build a wall in front – then throw them in. If you stack 'em in, the air can't get among 'em. Peats are like hay. Put 'em in a shed and they'll start to sweat, then dry out again.' Frost was the biggest enemy to any peats left outdoors. Soaked, they froze, swelling to twice their normal thickness. Peats were transported from storage on the moss to a site near the house in instalments of 1,000 or so. Jim said that 7,000 peats were sufficient for his cottage. Each peat brought into the house for the fire was broken into two, lengthways. He burnt the peat with wood, preferably ash. Peat tends to be a dusty fuel, 'but it's clean dust'. The old peat fireplace had an ash-hole underneath that was cleaned out once a week, the ash making a good fertiliser for the garden.

Bob Longmire of Bouth, who was born before the First World War, remembered when farms at the mouth of the Rusland Valley had their *peat dykes*: 'It's all peat dyke from Blind Beck to the new road.' As summer waned, cart after cart laden with peat could be seen moving along the winding roads to where it would be stacked near at hand. As school lads, Bob and his pals smoked peat, making the bowl of a simple pipe from the stem of elderberry, having removed the pith. The stem of the pipe was fashioned from a piece of honeysuckle. 'You put some peat in the bowl and drew on it. It was hot stuff. It nearly burnt your tongue off.' Every farm had a pair of bellows to coax a slumbering peat fire into life at daybreak. Dixons of Underfield owned the peat-ground and a farmer paid a few shillings extra rent to cover the peat workings. While Bob Longmire's brother was out of work owing to the closure of the gunpowder works, he hurried home one day and said to his sister, 'Give me plenty o' food and a can o' tea.' 'Why? Have you got a job somewhere?' asked the sister. 'Aye – it's cutting peat for Ted Jackson.' 'How long are you working?' The unexpected reply was: 'Right through till midnight.'

White blossom that characterises the Winster Valley in spring adorns the innumerable thorn trees. Canon H.D. Rawnsley, a Lakeland cleric who was one of the founders of the National Trust and an incessant scribbler, urged those who wished to see unspoiled Westmorland to take a carriage from Grange, Kendal or Windermere and explore the Winster Valley in May. To hear of Damson Saturday in Kendal was one thing; to see the fruit on the trees 'and the happy folk gathering their harvest' was another. He recorded that tons of damsons were bought 'to make a peculiar purple dye for the tanners'. At that time (1911), except in rare seasons of plenty, the fruit went to the jam-makers. Rawnsley also ventured to Cartmel Fell Chapel, dedicated to St Anthony, which he inevitably described as 'quaint' and 'old-world'. The east window with its fragments of 14th-century glass had probably come from Cartmel Priory.

At Lindale, which is reached by taking the Grange turn-off on the road to Barrow, John Wilkinson, ironmaster, is commemorated by a prominent monument made of iron. Wilkinson, whose achievements are now recognised as having been crucial in the Industrial Revolution, was taught iron-making in the 1730s by Isaac, his father, who was a furnaceman at Backbarrow, by the River Leven. Isaac started on his own account by the River Winster, having his ore and iron pigs borne by coastal barge along the Winster channel. His son, who became known as 'Iron-Mad' Wilkinson, provided James Watt with a cylinder 'bored to truth', enabling Watt, at long last, to make his revolutionary steam engine. Built at Wilkinson's works in Shropshire, this powerful, economical engine helped to create the industrial innovation that changed society.

88   *A farmhouse in Lyth Valley, a village*
drained by the River Gilpin.

At Lindale, one ponders John Wilkinson's other life. He bought Holme Island in 1765, an islet standing where the Winster flowed into the Bay, and built a three-storey house, complete with a tower, giving it the grand title of Castle Head. The grounds were landscaped and a 'secret garden' was built on the hill. A bridge gave him access to the mainland. But despite his brilliance, local people mistrusted him. He actually condoned work on Sundays and, when those involved in landscaping refused their labour, Irish workers were hired. The Irishmen, using large baskets, were set to work carrying earth to the summit of the island. Wilkinson was also derided because of his violation of the moral code. Immorality was rampant in his day but Wilkinson, always a blunt sort of man, tended to flaunt his mistress. On the credit side, he converted marshland into good arable land and kept sheep of a quality that impressed Arthur Young, who was travelling about the country, writing about rural matters. He made efforts to improve breeds of cattle and, as a prominent landowner, implemented the Enclosure Acts of the mid-18th century.

He died on the mainland in July 1808 and in due course was buried on Holme Island. He had blasted out spaces in living rock as burial places for himself and his family and had had several iron coffins made, each complete with a spanner. One was for his use; the others he tried to press on to friends. A story, related by P.J. Birch

89   *Harvesting damsons*
in Lyth Valley. The fruit is
usually ready for picking
in early September.

90   *Peat-cutting, Witherslack Moss. The inexpensive fuel was cut in May and had dried by October.*

of Lindale was that he died in France, having with him on his trip an iron coffin that proved too small to accommodate his remains. He was buried for a while until a larger coffin was made in England, whereupon the body was brought back to this country and interred at the old Midlands home. Eventually, Wilkinson was re-interred at Castle Head. His huge fortune was frittered away in litigation between his next of kin and his 'natural' family.

In 1832 John Fitchett of Warrington was the owner of a shooting lodge and stables on Holme Island. John Brogden, who was prominently connected with the Ulverston to Lancaster railway, purchased the island in 1851 and tethered it to the mainland via a causeway, which diverted the Winster channel to the eastern side. Brogden's second son, Alexander, enlarged the house, added a 'Temple of Vesta' and arranged for a vast quantity of soil to be transported to the grounds. Holme Island became well wooded. Among the uncommon trees was, inevitably, a Wellingtonia. Shrubs were planted and greenhouses constructed for the most delicate plants. Edward Mucklow, who took over the property in the early 1860s, added a veranda, farm and stable complex. Some of the exotic species of tree he introduced to the grounds have survived.

When the Mucklows bought the estate they arranged for what remained of John Wilkinson to be removed to the churchyard. The parson would not permit burial in consecrated ground and the remains were laid to rest just outside. When, years later, the churchyard was extended, Wilkinson was absorbed into God's Acre. No records

91   *A monument at Lindale to John Wilkinson, ironmaster.*

survive of his burial but his widow was interred locally and there is a memorial to her in the church. The 40-ft-high cast-iron obelisk standing near the road at Lindale was brought here from Castle Head. A dedication plate testifies to Wilkinson's 'different works, in various parts of the kingdom', which 'are lasting testimonies to his unceasing labours. His life was spent in action for the benefit of man and, as he presumed humbly to hope, to the Glory of God.'

Castle Head was a Catholic seminary from 1909 until 1978. Many of its priests became missionaries in Africa. Subsequently it became first a residential school for Catholic boys, then a field centre. Since 1997 it has been part of the Field Studies Council. The road from Lindale to Grange-over-Sands offers views of an extensive golf course and limestone crags. Grange no longer looks over sand; the shore has been colonised by spartina grass.

Nine

CARTMEL PENINSULA

The old parish of Cartmel, 60 square miles in extent, is almost surrounded by water. To the north lies Windermere, the Leven is the westward border between Cartmel and Furness, and to the east flows the Winster. Miles of Cartmel's southern boundary are washed by the tides of Morecambe Bay. Cartmel has its own little watercourse with the strange name of Ea – an ancient term for 'water'. It flows through a sweet-and-sour landscape, following the line of a geological fault, with limestone to the east and Silurian slates, known locally as 'blue stone', to the west. Streams threading the wide, shallow vale of Cartmel have down-to-earth names: Clogger Beck, Middlefield Beck, Flow Beck, Muddy Pool. The vale has widely contrasting landforms ranging from marshy fields to knolls topped with groups of trees, from farmsteads with floriferous meadows to mini-mansions standing in manicured parkland.

The Enclosure Acts changed the face of Cartmel, as they did much of England. About 1768, local landowners used this legislation to improve the thousands of acres of overstocked commons, marshes and mosses. The Act relating to the parish of Cartmel was passed in 1796. Some of the roads were a by-product of enclosure, although even the best of them were chancy for travellers. When, early in the 18th century, the 1st Lord George Cavendish journeyed to his home at Holker Hall, so narrow and rutted was the way that his carriage could not be driven nearer than Cart Lane, west of Grange, about four miles short of his destination. The carriage was drawn

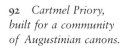

92 *Cartmel Priory,*
built for a community
of Augustinian canons.

93 *The tower of Cartmel Priory is unusual in having an extension that was set diagonally.*

over the beach to an old barn, where it remained until Lord George wished to return to London.

Canon Sam Taylor, author of *Cartmel: People and Priory*, told the author that the first thing to remember about the peninsula is that up to the time of the Romantic Movement – roughly the middle of the 18th century – this was probably the most secluded part of England. Students of romantic beauty, from Gilpin to Wordsworth, used Cartmel as a stepping-stone on their way to the Lakes. Canon Taylor spoke of the King of Northumbria, who influenced the development of Cartmel by his desire to pacify the country, to make it habitable and to evangelise it for Christianity. At the end of the seventh century, he gave the lands of Cartmel 'with all the Britons in it', to St Cuthbert, Bishop of Lindisfarne. Pacification on a grander scale came in 1188 with the arrival of the black-clad Canons Regular of St Augustine. The founder, William Marshall, Baron of Cartmel and Earl of Pembroke, also endowed the lowlands of Cartmel peninsula and the hill country of Cartmel Fell. In the priory charter was written:

This house I founded for the increase of Holy Religion, giving and conceding to it every kind of liberty that mouth can utter or the heart of man can conceive; whosoever therefore shall cause loss or injury to the said house or its inmates may he incur the curse of God and of the Blessed Virgin Mary and of all the other saints of God, besides my particular malediction.

A strange tale relates that the canons heard a voice telling them to build the priory on a spit of land between two streams that were flowing in opposite directions. How could this be? Arthur Freerson, a local historian, offered an explanation. The Ea flows southwards. To the east is Clogger Beck, which flows northwards from its source in a tarn at Pit Farm. In later times, water from this source was also directed along a cut to the south of the priory. Said Mr Freerson, 'This famous building is actually standing on an island.' Cartmel Priory, which looked more towards the Bay than the hills, was not an especially large monastery. The fabric and some of the fittings of the priory church remain to hint at its medieval splendour. It stands in grand isolation.

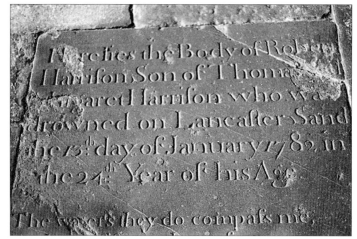

94 *Gravestone in Cartmel Priory relating to a fatility on the Sands.*

So, then, did the village. James Stockdale, antiquary, evoked the Cartmel of the mid-18th century, when it was 'cut off by mountains or thick woods from the rest of the world and had no passage over or through but clog-wheeled cart and packhorse tracks'. He also recalled the hideous sounds made by wooden carts: their crude, scantily greased mechanism created 'a most unnatural squeak ... disagreeable music ... about as pleasant as that produced by "the cleaver and marrow bones"'. Mercifully, the noise of modern traffic is subdued. Norman Nicholson described the village as ecclesiastic but not obviously on the road to anywhere. He told the improbable but entertaining story of the tradesman who, for years, passed within a hundred yards of Cartmel without discovering that it was there.

Not much happened between 1188 and the priory's dissolution in 1537. Tucked away from the gaze of the world, Cartmel was not greatly affected by raiding Scots early in the 14th century. Priors came and went; the canons lived their quiet spiritual lives, leaving others to cultivate the land. Then came the Dissolution. By an Act of 1536, monasteries with a worth of under £200 were to be confiscated. In an official valuation of property, Cartmel Priory was assessed at £91 6s. 3d. A fresh survey was secured which raised the valuation to £212 12s. 10½d. Nonetheless, the dissolution went ahead, with the Earls of Derby and Sussex appointed as the King's Commissioners. The land was considered to be valuable, as was the metal: not only the priory plate but also thick lead from the roof that had been cast on sand-beds rather than rolled out. The great bells were dropped and carted away. Unlike the

95 *Loaves on a shelf recall the old bread charity of Cartmel Priory.*

96 *Sidney Buckley,
artist, promoted Cartmel,
and especially its priory,
through his paintings.*

97   *This milestone at
Cartmel shows distances
'oversands'.*

Cistercians, the Black Canons remained as parish priests. Cartmel claimed parochial
rights, which, after a legal fight, were recognised by authority. The parishioners were
allowed to keep what is known to this day as the Town Choir but which originally
was the Chapel of St Michael.

   Saving an aisle eventually led to the restoration of the whole building by George
Preston, of Holker Hall. Within a century all was tidy again. Mr Preston adorned
the chancel 'with curious carved woodwork'. Happily, having been rescued only
60 years after it lost its roof, the priory church has a venerable appearance today,
although it has a mixture of styles, having been built during a period of transition
between Norman and Early English architecture, and also having had a necessary
restoration carried out in 1859. The cost was met by the 7th Duke of Devonshire.
When the tower was extended in 1410, the new masonry was placed diagonally, an
eccentric touch that distinguishes Cartmel from other great churches. The misericords,

of 15th-century date, are fascinating, the topics including a pelican in piety, a mermaid with two tails, an ape doctor, elephant and castle and, equally intriguing, a combination of oak tree and unicorn. Among the treasures of Cartmel Priory are listed one of the first umbrellas, which is over two centuries old, a Vinegar Bible of 1716 and the 1596 first edition of Spenser's *Faerie Queene* (a book stolen in 1929, taken to America, recovered, and returned to Cartmel in 1931). The chapel on Cartmel Fell, founded as a chapel-of-ease to Cartmel in 1504 and dedicated to St Anthony, continued to serve the former tenants of the priory, and became a separate parish in the 18th century.

Cartmel Priory church remains at the heart of the community. Cartmel itself is a picturesque huddle of buildings from the 17th to the 19th centuries, with a square complete with cross and pump. In high summer there is usually a log-jam of vehicles and a babble of voices here. The largest crowd appears on Whit Monday, when horse racing takes place on a course that is little more than an arrow flight from the market-place.

Grange-over-Sands

A current guidebook describes Grange as 'genteel' and presents it as 'an excellent example of a prosperous Edwardian seaside resort ... steeped in elegance and charm'. With a muddy shore and languid tides, it was not likely to appeal as a major holiday centre. Yet, sheltered from the north winds and open to most of the sunshine, it had an agreeably mild climate that would appeal to those who, having made money through trade and commerce, discovered the Furness Railway had brought the area within second-home range. The charms of this 'Torquay of the North', and a nucleus of new settlers determined to keep Grange genteel, led to many of them retiring here.

98 *A romantic view of Grange-over-Sands, which, early in the 19th century, appealed to early visitors because of its rocks and inlets.*

99 *Pleasure boats from Morecambe used this pier at Grange-over-Sands.*

100 *A sale bill of 1811.*

To be LET or SOLD,

BY PRIVATE TREATY,

AND ENTERED UPON IMMEDIATELY;

ALL THAT WELL-BUILT COMMODIOUS

Dwelling-house,

SITUATE AT GRANGE,

IN THE PARISH OF CARTMEL AND COUNTY OF LANCASTER,

late in the Possession of John Moreland, *Esq.*

CONSISTING of a Dining-Room, two Parlours, a large Kitchen, Pantry, Brew-house, two Cellars on the First-floor, two Stair-cases, seven Lodging-Rooms and Closets on the Second-floor, a large Room in the Attic which may be converted into two or three Lodging-Rooms, a large Cistern supplying the House with Rain-water, and a Pump near the Door, an useful Garden and valuable Orchard bearing excellent Fruit, a good Stable, Cow-house, two Coach-houses, Barn and other suitable Out-buildings.

Grange had a modest beginning. In the Cartmel Priory Registers of 1536 it is referred to in relation to the Bay, the title being 'Grange with Kentisbank'. The words 'Carters Lonnye Crossing', which appear on the John Speed map of Lancashire (1577), further emphasise the connection between Grange and the oversands route. A grange was an outlying monastic property, but by the time of the 1851 census this outlier of Cartmel Priory had become a farm occupied by John Brough, his wife Isabella, and Mary, their infant daughter. At that time there were 40 houses, 188 people and no fishermen.

Little is known about Grange before the early part of the 19th century, by which time its rocks and inlets were attracting discerning holidaymakers. Bathers were attended to by Fanny Wright, whose head was adorned by 'a wonderful poke bonnet and, underneath it, a much befrilled night-cap, the like of which one sees no more'. An old man walked from Lindale to Grange daily with letters in the crown of his capacious hat. Being unable to read or write, he was happy when people picked out letters intended for them. Peggy Keith, the carrier, who brought provisions from Kendal, smoked a short black pipe and always wore a man's coat 'in preference to more womanly attire'. One dark night, alas, she fell from her cart and died.

An editorial in the *Ulverston Advertiser* in March 1852 foresaw that 'when the railway is completed and the medicinal virtues of the spa of Holywell [at Humphrey Head] are taken into consideration … this place will doubtless become a favourite resort both as a sea-bathing and watering place'. The charms of the village were becoming known even before the arrival of the railway. In June 1811, when a 'commodious dwelling house' was advertised, it was stated that the premises adjoined the seashore 'and command

101   *Promenade at Grange-over-Sands, which now overlooks a prairie of spartina grass.*

an extensive view of the whole Bay. There is an excellent bathing place. Vessels are frequently seen sailing under the windows, to and from Liverpool, Glasgow, etc.'

The Furness Railway arrived in August 1857. W.E. Swale, in his story of 'a gentle township', described the end of a 'long age of innocence'. More, and larger, hotels and hydros arose. Piers were built to serve sailing vessels and steamers that arrived from across the Bay. 'With Lancashire and Yorkshire manufacturing centres brought within two hours by rail, rich textile men began to settle in the town. The flow of day trippers and holidaymakers steadily increased.' The railway company opened the *Grange Hotel*, with Thomas Rigg as the first manager. Carriages and post-horses were available for hire. In summer, coach tours to Lakeside were organised. A writer in the *Westmorland Gazette* in March 1867 observed that, 'It is in the character of a sanatorium that Grange is growing and will flourish ... It is not fast nor boisterous nor overcrowded like some places one might name; it has neither bathing vans nor donkeys.' Grange spread up a steep hillside, offering almost every home a panoramic view of Morecambe Bay and the restless tides.

Mid-19th-century visitors to Grange were able to watch fishermen fixing their nets on stakes of around two feet, so that when the tide ebbed they might recover 'flukes, plaice, sometimes even a salmon'. Women and children earned a scant living by cockling on the sands. They gathered together in a barn near the shore

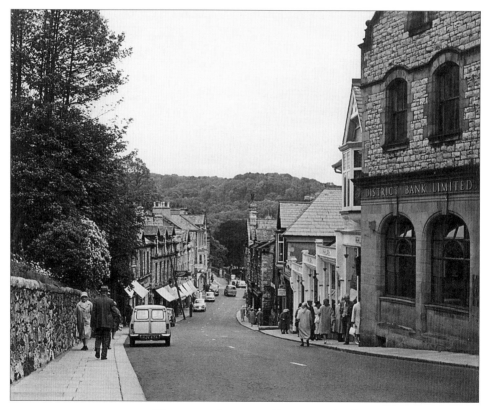

102   *The steep main street at Grange-over-Sands.*

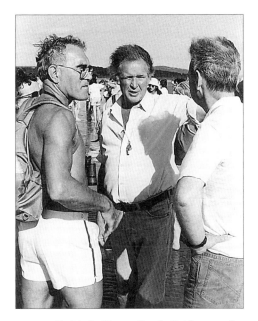

103   *Cedric Robinson, Sands Guide, one of the best-known residents of Grange.*

104   *William Burrows, former Guide to the Sands, was also a fisherman.*

to dispose of their catch to merchants. The women were bronzed to a copper hue. Their ragged children had hair that was rough and the colour of asses' hides. Young women, strong and muscular, 'drenched with wet, crowded with their baskets in the candlelight, measuring out their lots to the dealer'. Cockles supplemented many a meal, being fried in rows on a gridiron till the shells opened, by which time they were done to perfection. Vinegar and pepper were added. The cockles were eaten with bread and butter. In later times, they were boiled, shelled and made into a large paté.

Canon H.R. Smith, incumbent from 1858 until 1888, suggested the place should be known as Grange-over-Sands to avoid confusion with Grange-in-Borrowdale. Or could it have been a ploy to attract visitors? In *John Heywood's Guide* (1891) it was pointed out that Grange had a 'high reputation for respectability and dignified repose. This is not a paradise of burnt-cork artists, of German bands, of galloping and reckless trippers; it is not in fact a bathing-place in the ordinary sense.'

The Clock Tower on Church Hill was a gift from Mrs Dearden. She first offered it to the railway company, who declined it. This being Grange, it was arranged that the bells in the tower would not operate from 11 p.m. until 6 a.m. A selection of exotic trees and shrubs, plus a pond for waterfowl, beautified Grange. Flowerbeds were set on the promenade in 1910.

That was the year when steamers that had plied their trade between Grange and Morecambe vacated the wooden piers. Grange folk had gone to Morecambe 'on the morning tide' and stopped there all day; the Morecambe folk came 'with the tide' and had to go back with it, which gave them scarcely any time to look around. The

105 *Abbot Hall, Kents Bank, is owned by Christian Guild Holidays.*

106 *This inn at Allithwaite, near Grange, is named after the Sands Guide.*

fare was cheap, and so (the Grange residents of the time might have thought) were the exuberant holidaymakers from Lancashire and Yorkshire towns who flooded the town, finding nothing much to do. Cross-bay sailings in *Yorkshire Lass* and *Morecambe Queen* ended because of the shifting of the channels, a consequence of the construction of a causeway to Holme Island and the railway viaduct over the Kent estuary. Holidaymakers at Grange could be rowed into the Bay to ride an incoming tide. There were many 'lazy' tides, with little perceptible movement. Years ago, the morning tide spilled over broad flats and had a silvery sheen and the Bay would dry out to a yellowish hue that changed subtly with the passing hours. Today, instead of sand and mud, there is a prairie of spartina grass.

Abbot Hall, a typical gentleman's house, stands in its own grounds five minutes' walk from a railway station at Kents Bank. It was built on part of a tract of land once owned by Furness Abbey. Ninety years ago the property came into the ownership of Methodist Guild Holidays as 'a charming holiday centre for young Methodists', the premises being 'lighted throughout with electric light on the most modern lines'. The original guesthouse at Kents Bank – a house named Moorhurst – had received useful publicity in an article that appeared in *The Methodist Recorder* in 1910. Kents Bank was described as being on 'the South Coast of Northern England'. Hardy young holidaymakers from Abbot Hall, having had the proverbial hearty breakfast, set off on foot or by train for a day in the open air, returning for another substantial meal. The Wesley Guild became Methodist Guild Holidays and is now Christian Guild Holidays. All are welcome.

Seeing Humphrey Head for the first time, you might be pardoned for thinking that a huge grey whale was stranded on the low-lying northern shores of Morecambe Bay. So few sea cliffs exists on the Cumbrian coast that when one is encountered you cannot keep your eyes off it, even if it is only 160 feet high. Behind the headland are woods and hedge-bordered fields, some of which are ploughed. The Fairy Chapel is a natural cave tenanted by jackdaws. A local tradition, which was of course versified, insisted that 'the last wolf' was slain on Humphrey Head. When the hunt took place is not known for certain, but Sir John Harrington of Wraysholme Tower was the hero of the chase and he was interred in Cartmel Priory.

Humphrey Head had a celebrated holy well, though the water was 'a bit brakky … not so good at first tasting'. In the late 18th and 19th centuries the Holy Well of St Agnes, which had once been a venerated possession of Cartmel Priory, gave this headland considerable renown. Thomas West, author of *The Antiquaries of Furness* (1805), called it a 'medicinal spring' and was the first to mention the 'brakky' state of the water. Much frequented in summer, the water was 'a good remedy for worms'.

It was bottled for distribution, regular supplies being taken to the lead miners on Alston Moor. Milk kits full of water were transported to Morecambe and sold to holidaymakers. The well, marked by some crumbled masonry, has lost its power to charm if not to cure. The main tonic today comes from using Humphrey Head as a vantage point for the wide-sweeping Bay. Care should be exercised on the cliff, an inscribed stone emphasising this point with the words: 'Beware how you these rocks ascend/Here William Pedder met his end.' Among the more unusual sights seen by the author was that of a fisherman in a rowing boat with a tractor in tow. When his tractor was bogged down in soft sand, a dozen 40-gallon drums were attached to it for buoyancy. Said the fisherman: 'I tried to pull her out with a rope but it kept snagging. So I went for my boat and towed the tractor back to the shore.'

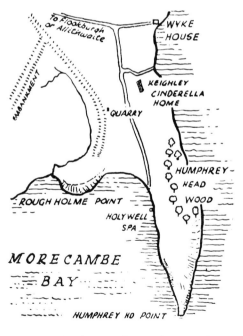

107   *Sketch map of Humphrey Head.*

108   *Holker, an estate village on an estate flanking the Bay.*

To the west of Humphrey Head, but still in sight of it, was the compact community of Ravenstown, consisting of 200 houses laid out around a village green. It sprang into life in the First World War, when Vickers of Barrow-in-Furness hoped to reclaim some land to support mooring masts for an airship project. As the land proved unsuitable for this purpose the airship base was never developed. Ravenstown languished like a beached whale, having 'one road in and t'same road out'. The streets were named after battles: Jutland, Marne, Somme and Arras.

Holker Hall

The road to the old park at Holker forms part of the Flookburgh parish boundary. Holker (pronounced Hooker) is the stately home of Lord and Lady Cavendish. Representatives of this family have occupied Holker for four centuries, their emblem being a snake with the motto *Cavendo Tutus*, a pun that might be translated as 'safety through caution' – or look before you leap! At Holker a strikingly attractive Victorian mansion, with 22 acres of formal and woodland gardens and 120 acres of park containing red and fallow deer, has been 'open to view' for over half a century.

Holker, owned by Cartmel Priory at the Dissolution, was annexed to the Duchy of Lancaster, and subsequently transferred to the Bishopric of Chester. In about 1556 the property was purchased by the Preston family, and in 1604 George Preston built himself a fine house and also paid for the restoration of Cartmel Priory. The Prestons had marital links with the Lowthers, a Preston heiress having married Sir William Lowther of Marske, Yorkshire. Lord George Augustus Cavendish, who inherited Holker in 1756, was an M.P. who became 'Father' of the Commons. He engaged John Carr of York to add a new 'elegant modern gothic' east wing and considerably modified the appearance of the grounds. In about 1815 the house was faced with Roman cement. Lord George was created Earl of Burlington and his grandson, William Cavendish, the 2nd Earl, became the 7th Duke of Devonshire. Between 1838 and 1842 the house was given a Gothic appearance by the architect, Webster of Kendal. A new stable block was also built.

The 7th Duke (1808-91), with over 6,000 acres in Furness and Cartmel making him one of the largest landowners in the area, had a special fondness for Holker, which was just one of six family seats. Far from being indolent, as were some men of property, the Duke involved himself with many aspects of local life and also set trends. When local farmers with arable farms were unable to compete in quality and price with imported grain, the Duke populated his Holker estate with beef cattle. As the owner of big slate quarries, he associated himself with the industrial development of Barrow. His association with the Furness Railway led to his having a private coach when travelling. In March 1871 fire destroyed the west wing of Holker Hall but it was promptly rebuilt on a grander scale, using local materials and estate timber, the architects being Paley and Austin of Lancaster. The rooms were sumptuously furnished. The mansion stands in 22 acres of garden wherein is a fountain, water from which flows down a cascade; it is a smaller version of the great cascade at Chatsworth, the celebrated home of the Devonshires in Derbyshire.

The Holker estate extends to the Leven. The river Leven has its source with the outflow of Windermere, which was anciently divided into three cables or *cubbles*. The low cable extended from below the ferry to Newby Bridge, which had long been an important crossing point. Years ago, when the manager of the *Swan Hotel* at Newby Bridge inadvertently intruded, the District Council, owners of the lake-bed, asserted that their jurisdiction extended to the bridge. The river begins as a brawling watercourse, turning white with fury as it forces its way between boulders on stretches beloved by canoeists.

109 *Holker Hall, home of Lord and Lady Cavendish.*

110 *The Victorian grandeur of Holker Hall.*

A short distance below Newby Bridge, an eel trap was attached to a race that fed water to a 10-hp undershot wheel at the local mill, which dated back to 1470. When three-year-old elvers were running upriver to Windermere in spring they could surmount the weir via a 'fish ladder'. In Windermere they grew into yellow eels, dining mainly on snails and insect larvae. The silvery appearance was assumed just before they began their return journey to the sea. The main run of eels, in August and September, was at the start of a migratory journey of about 3,000 miles to the vast breeding grounds of the Sargasso Sea. The fish moved under cover of night in wild, wet conditions. They were uneasy even in moonlight. Eels carried along by the water were held up by a wooden grid and directed by a smaller quantity of water into a wooden box, five feet long by two feet wide and two feet high. A larger box was sunk in the ground nearby to store eels taken from the trap until sufficient had been gathered for them to be consigned by rail to Manchester. Fifty years ago H. Leck, who had taken over from John and William Knowles, was operating the trap. It was known for a nightly catch to consist of from two to three hundredweight of eels.

Greenodd, the northernmost port on Morecambe Bay, had an increase in trade in 1819 with the opening of a turnpike road between Levens Bridge and Ulverston, but its advantage was lost when the Furness Railway was completed. Much of the road had been 'floated' on bundles of juniper taken from Whitbarrow. The income from two tollgates enabled the trustees to cope with the wear and tear of countless horse-drawn vehicles. Where their road crossed the mosses, the wheels of wood-wagons cut through the thin surface. John Kellett, writing of the railway in the first half of the 19th century, reported that a 'hive of industry' had sadly been destroyed 'by that cruel Iron Horse that has been the ruin of many other village industries and small seaports'. In recent times Greenodd has been bypassed by the road to Barrow, and what was the main street is now a cul-de-sac.

Ten

ULVERSTON AND THE COAST ROAD

At La'al Oosten, as Ulverston is affectionately known by its older residents, an observant traveller notices a change of architectural mood. The town stands on the division between limestone and slate. Some buildings were constructed using the pretty grey rock, as at Grange, when (wrote Norman Nicholson) 'the limestone goes on the razzle'. Other buildings, of a duller grey, do not lack architectural pretension, the most exuberant being the vast railway station. Ulverston was the capital of old-time Furness because of its geographical position: at the focal point of important land routes, and at one end of the oversands route linking Furness with the outer world. Dalton had been the important town in monastic times; now, with Furness Abbey closed at the whim of the king, it was Ulverston that attracted the attention.

Ulverston attained its market town status in 1280 with the award of a Royal Charter by Edward I. The town has its picturesque corners but, overall, is a workaday place. A boom period began in the latter part of the 18th century and continued into the 19th. By mid-century the population had reached 50,000 and during Ulverston's heyday it became the main social centre of Lancashire North of the Sands. The hiring fair attracted interest over a wide area. The gentry built their town houses at the outskirts and attended the theatre or the grand balls. Sea captains associated with the ship canal had their homes here, where they rested between voyages.

Professional folk, including lawyers, also congregated. Early in the 19th century, John Audland, who had just lost a local law-suit, wrote a poem that included the lines:

> But t'Divil himself
> Mead lawyers and 'tornies,
> And pleac'd 'em at Ooston an' Dotan [Dalton] i' Furniss.

Later that century, the town, in common with others at the time, suffered badly from overcrowding and poor sanitation. There were no proper sewers or drains, and 'fevers prevail in the houses of the poor'. Since the 1840s it had not been a good time for trade either. Ulverston was exporting workers, many of them seeking employment in the mills of Preston. Girls who left school with little alternative employment to domestic labour were hired as servant lasses on the farms, some travelling to adjacent counties. The most fortunate of the servant girls married farmers' sons.

Ulverston's market-place, little changed from times past, is busiest when the Thursday market takes place. The oldest building in town is St Mary's Church, which

111   *Market Street, Ulverston, a town once noted for the fair at which farm servants were hired.*

112   *Ulverston's old crest, reflecting its iron smelting, farming and maritime connection through a ship canal.*

113 *County Square, Ulverston. The town became a notable commercial centre.*

has been much altered over the centuries but retains some 12th-century stonework. Armorial bearings reflect aspects of the town's long history. The modern crest, rising from a gold coronet, has three visible roses of Lancaster. A black wolf stands for the name of the town, 'Wulf-heres-tun', the flames emerging from its mouth symbolising iron smelting. Agriculture is represented by a golden sheaf. On a shield are yet older symbols: the red bars on white that form part of the arms of the de Lancasters, and crosiers to represent Furness Abbey and Conishead Priory. A black portion, fretted in white, is plucked from the Harrington arms; the Barrow family's arms are represented by an anchor and fleur-de-lis.

Ulverston's continuing status as a market town did enable it to avoid the worst rigours of industrial depression in the 1930s, and the arrival of new industries later brought it prosperity. The town has kept its pride in the great men of the past. A scaled down version of the Eddystone lighthouse, which has stood atop Hoad Hill since 1850, commemorates the achievements of John Barrow (1764-1848), a local lad who found fame and acquired a knighthood during a career as a naval administrator and traveller. He was a founder member of the Royal Geographical Society and, for 40 years, held the office of Second Secretary to the Admiralty. The anchor on the town's coat of arms witnesses Ulverston's role as a port, which it undertook in 1796 when John Rennie of Lancaster devised a mile-long canal capable of taking seagoing vessels. The initial estimate of the cost, £2,000, was superseded by the final figure of £3,083. The canal extended across the peat mosses that, along with the commons and wasteland, had been transformed by an Enclosure Act.

114 *This mock lighthouse on Hoad Hill commemorates Sir John Barrow, naval administrator.*

115 *A sign at Canal Foot. Ulverston won recognition as a port in 1796.*

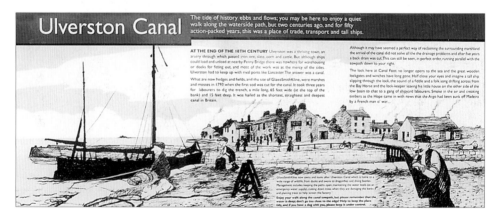

Ulverston's ship canal throve until, in Victorian times, the trade seeped away to Barrow. The ship canal was closed to vessels in 1944 and was eventually sealed off, becoming a source of fresh water for Glaxo Laboratories. Now known as GlaxoSmithKline, and one of the world's leading research-based pharmaeutical and healthcare companies, the firm celebrated 50 years of association with the town in 1998. A reminder of the anniversary is an ornate iron seat in a prominent position at Canal Foot, from which there is a panoramic view of Morecambe Bay, including the Leven railway viaduct and tiny Chapel Island. In recent times, Lord Birkett, a distinguished advocate, who was born and raised locally, used his keen mind and silver tongue to save Ullswater from over-exploitation by Manchester waterworks. At the other end of the social scale, Arthur Stanley Jefferson, much better known as Stan Laurel, emigrated to America and, with Oliver Hardy, became a bumbling, taciturn film star of world renown.

A hall at Swarthmoor, a short distance from Ulverston, developed strong associations with Quakerism. George Fox, a 'seeker after truth', came to Swarthmoor in 1652. Fox had climbed Pendle Hill and, looking northwards, saw a great crowd of people gathered there. At Swarthmoor he met Margaret Fell, the wife of a local judge, who at the time of that first visit was away from home. Judge Fell permitted Fox and his supporters, his wife Margaret and her daughters, and some pious folk known as 'Westmorland Seekers', to use Swarthmoor Hall, which had been built by the Fell family in 1586, for their meetings. They became known collectively as Friends or Quakers.

Margaret Fell, who was born at Marsh Grange, a manor house some seven miles away, grew up with great physical as well as spiritual strength. Her husband's power and position as a judge was enough to protect the Friends from the law, but when he

116   *Remains of lock gates on the 18th-century ship canal.*

117   *Canal Foot. The ship canal, closed to boats in 1944, was eventually sealed off.*

118   *Morecambe Bay from Canal Foot.*

119   *A Victorian garden party at Stone Cross, Ulverston.*

died six years later they endured much persecution. Margaret's faith was not impaired by imprisonment in Lancaster. She refused to ban religious meetings at Swarthmoor and thought nothing, as a middle-aged lady, of crossing Morecambe Bay on horseback to catch the London coach from Lancaster. She went directly to the King, and was thus instrumental in the release of many Quaker prisoners. Eleven years after the death of Judge Fell, Margaret and George Fox were married in Bristol.

The Meeting House built at Swarthmoor was a gift from Fox who, being an inveterate traveller, spent little time in the area himself. In 1660, having been arrested at Swarthmoor, he was conducted on the oversands route by a troop of horsemen to trial and imprisonment in Lancaster Castle. He visited Swarthmoor two years before his death at the age of 68. Fox was interred in Bunhill Fields, the nonconformist burial ground in London, and Margaret, his wife, was buried alongside others in a small enclosure on Birkrigg Common, a burial place with an ingenious swinging gate that lets sheep in and out at will.

Edwin Waugh was one of thousands of visitors to Swarthmoor Hall, and described it as 'a large, irregular Elizabethan building, with nothing grand about it ... The doorways are small; some of the windows are built up; and it has

120   *Swarthmoor Hall, home of Judge Fell and his wife Margaret, became a notable centre of Quakerism.*

121　*Conishead Priory, a vast Victorian building designed for Col Braddyll.*

altogether a bald appearance considering its size and former importance'. Its setting nonetheless impressed him. Swarthmoor looked over quiet fields 'with a kind of ascetic solemnity, as if it was mingling dreams of the past with a patient waiting for the result of slow decay'. He walked to the Meeting House, about a mile away, and found Friends had gathered there in silent worship. 'There was no sound but that of the sea-breeze whistling over the fields of Swarthmoor.'

Coast Road to Barrow

A hospital for the poor built beside the Leven estuary in 1160 became Conishead Priory, dedicated to the Virgin Mary and attended by black-robed Augustinian canons. Inevitably there were disputes between the priory and the mighty Furness Abbey. While the status of Ulverston was being argued over in 1230, the canons of Conishead won the right to administer both the village and Pennington, whereas Furness had to be content with Dalton and Urswick. Conishead maintained a guide to supervise crossings of the Leven estuary from Canal Foot to Sandgate, near Flookburgh. Though much narrower than Kent Sands, the Leven estuary was considered to be the more dangerous of the two. It is said that Conishead stationed a priest on Chapel Island, a fleck of land 250 yards long and 50 yards across.

122　*Buddhist temple at Conishead, in the grounds of the old priory.*

123 *Chapel Island, in the estuary of the River Leven.*

124 *Mock ruins on Chapel Island. They are relatively modern, having been built for effect.*

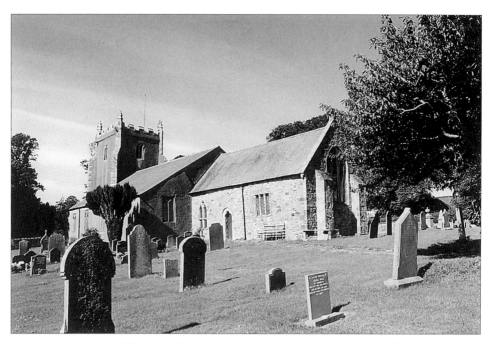

125 *Aldingham Church, protected from the sea by a stout wall.*

After the Dissolution Lord Monteagle built 'a tolerable gentleman's house' on the site. In size and style it did not match its grandiose successor, designed for Col Thomas Richard Gale Braddyll (1776-1862), who succeeded to the estate in 1818. Braddyll, who inherited a fortune, commissioned the architect Philip Wyatt to rebuild the house and the work was carried out between 1821 and 1836. The result was breathtaking: a mansion in the gothic style, with two octagonal towers, each 100 feet high. The rooms of the new Conishead were elegantly furnished, and the walls were decked with fine paintings. Chapel Island was provided with sham ruins in 1823, a delight for visiting 'pleasure parties', who might then buy refreshments from a fisherman and his wife at the adjacent cottage. Income was derived from a pier near Bardsea, one of several loading points for iron ore being shipped to South Wales. In his prime Braddyll presided over the Ulverston Canal Company and was highly placed in local society. He had a major shareholding in a coal company in Durham but later ran into financial difficulties; in 1854, the priory and 800 acres of land were sold to Henry Askew, who added a clock tower, stables and cottage.

In its Victorian heyday the house had a small army of servants, and woodmen who attended to 50 varieties of tree, including Lebanon Cedar, California Redwood and a Wellingtonia. Conishead passed through a number of hands before 1878, when a Scottish syndicate purchased it, along with 150 acres. It then became a hydropathic hotel with accommodation for 240 guests. Four years later the Durham Miners' Welfare Committee bought the priory for £35,000 and spent another £22,000 converting it into a convalescent home. It remained thus until 1976, when the Manjushri Institute purchased the hall and 70 acres of land. Conishead became a Buddhist centre.

The vast building, having stood empty and neglected for five years, was riddled with dry rot. As it was a listed building, restoration work had to conform to the original style, which included decorative ceilings, a vaulted great hall complete with stained glass windows, and a cloister corridor of enormous length. Few of the 80 rooms were left untouched as tons of wood, brick and plaster were ripped away so that fungicide might be injected into the walls affected by rot. Steel was shaped and welded to replace rotten beams and much of the roof was replaced, the new guttering taking the form of moulded fibreglass. Contrasting with the gothic-style hall is the Kadampa World Peace Temple, which was based on a traditional Buddhist design.

Bardsea, with its spired church, lies on the hill above the Coast Road to Barrow and is best known for its splendid beach. The Coast Road, constructed during the inter-war years by out-of-work miners from Lindal and Ulverston, together with redundant workers from the munitions factories of Barrow, cuts through a low part of the Sea Wood. Now owned by the Woodland Trust, this remnant of old

126   *St Cuthbert, patron saint of Aldingham.*

127   *Tombstones set beside the churchyard wall at Aldingham.*

128   *Gleaston Castle, built by the le Flemings in the Manor of Muchland.*

129   *Great Urswick, a village set beside a lake.*

Furness is composed of oak and ash that grow from cracks in limestone. Ringed by secondary roads, one of them beginning at the Sea Wood, and criss-crossed by public footpaths, Birkrigg Common is easily accessible, long stretches of road being unfenced. Sheep keep the grass short and fresh between expanses of bracken, the fronds of which are green in summer and have an attractive coppery tint in winter. Birkrigg is a vantage point for Morecambe Bay. The standing stones known as a Druid's Circle, although they are certainly older than that, were used for cremations, some ashes being found in a collared urn.

The dedication of Aldingham church to St Cuthbert has been attributed to the ninth-century flight of the monks of Lindisfarne, seeking to protect the saint's coffin from Danes who were ravaging the east coast. Perhaps they hoped to take the coffin to Ireland and bad weather forced them to turn back. In due course Cuthbert

130   *Aldingham Hall, built by a former rector, Dr John Stonard, in 1816.*

would have his resting place in Durham. When Domesday scribes made their survey in 1086, the manor was held by a Saxon lord named Emulf; it was subsequently granted by the Crown to Roger de Poitou but the Crown retrieved it when Roger committed treason. Henry II, lord of Furness, granted Aldingham and a great deal of land to William le Fleming. David, a member of the same family, became the first rector in 1180. After the Dissolution of the Monasteries Aldingham acquired two bells but records do not show whether they had been hung at Furness Abbey or Conishead Priory.

Now bypassed by the Coast Road, the church and rectory of Aldingham are protected from the depredations of the sea by a stout nine-foot wall erected by a former rector, Dr John Stonard, in 1816. He officiated from 1814 until 1849, restoring a church that had been largely unchanged since the 15th century. It was unfortunate that he arranged for the oak

131   *The font in Great Urswick church.*

132 *Drawing of an ancient stone, Great Urswick church.*

beams supporting the roof to be covered by a low flat ceiling. When he preached from his three-decker pulpit his head was within 15 inches of it. Dr Stonard's great wealth became legendary. In 1849 he built the imposing Aldingham Hall, which lies across the road from the church, and bequeathed the hall and his fortune to his butler, E.J. Shollick, who had saved his life on the Sands. The grateful butler added the name Stonard to the Christian names of each of his six sons. Shollick lived at Aldingham until 1867, when he moved to Highgate, in north London. John Macaulay, brother of Lord Macaulay, the historian, was the incumbent from 1849 until 1879.

The parish of Aldingham, in Low Furness, undulates gently. Material left when glacial ice melted formed rounded hills known as drumlins. At Gleaston, a castle built by the le Flemings consisted of four square towers, connected by strong curtain walls. One of the towers has disappeared; the other three are ruined. The possessions of Michael le Fleming were the only lands in all Furness exempt from the grant that King Stephen made to Furness Abbey, hence the title Manor of Muchland (Michael's Land). A hidden treasure is Gleaston Water Mill, which is still operational and has an 18-ft waterwheel, an 11-ft wooden pit wheel and an assembly of venerable pieces of machinery from the 18th century. The main source of water comes from Gleaston Beck via a watercourse that is two-thirds of a mile long. In the summer months the watercourse dries up; the mill then relies on two springs. In its heyday Gleaston was mainly an oats mill so there is a drying kiln. By the 18th century, however, wheat was becoming popular and one pair of stones was dedicated purely to wheat production, the other two pairs continuing to grind oats.

Eleven

BARROW-IN-FURNESS

The Abbot of Furness held a market and fair at Dalton, which was the Daltune of Domesday Book. Ere long Dalton became the abbey's administrative centre. When Barrow was still an insignificant coastal settlement, the parish of Dalton sprawled over 17,961 acres, taking in the islands. In 1867 up-and-coming Barrow was incorporated as a municipal borough, and by 1881 the parish of Dalton had shrunk to 7,223 acres, though it retained its importance as the main centre for the mining of haematite (iron ore). Compact, grey-roofed and tucked away in a narrow valley, out of sight of the sea, Dalton has the touch of antiquity that is lacking from the adjacent boom-town of Barrow, where there is a grid-iron pattern of wide streets and the major thoroughfares bear the names of Victorian industrialists.

Dalton's redstone parish church, dedicated to St Mary, is like a mini-cathedral and has preserved fragments of stained glass from Furness Abbey. In the churchyard, which is large, flat and apt to be overlooked, is a slab covering the remains of George Romney, 18th-century portrait painter, who was born at Dalton in 1734, the son of a cabinet-maker. George's career as an artist began when, aged 21, he was apprenticed to a travelling portrait painter, but he went on to achieve national acclaim. Behind the market cross is the blocky red form of Dalton Castle, so called despite looking more like a pele tower. Initially comprising four floors and walls up to six feet thick, this 'guardian of Furness' had a prime position at the approach to Furness Abbey. The original structure suffered badly when the Scots arrived in 1322. In its long and chequered history it has been a courthouse and, until 1774, a prison. Here were kept Parliamentary prisoners from the Civil War. The Court Leet was held at Dalton Castle until 1925. Under its present owners, the National Trust, who obtained the title from the Duke of Buccleuch, the castle was restored in the late 1960s and, more recently, has been provided with a new roof.

Clog irons and red earth at Dalton symbolised the hetic age when ironstone was mined. Pastor West, author of *Antiquities of Furness*, who lived in Dalton, aptly called the district the 'Peru of Furness'. Carts lumbering from Dalton to Barrow left a broad red stain on the roads to mark their progress. Our old friend Edwin Waugh found in this neighbourhood roads, houses, cattle and men that were all more or less coloured with oxide of iron. 'A Furness miner, when disguised in his Sunday clothes, is seldom slow to tell you that he has "ta'en his degrees i'th'Red Lone College".' In some areas of pure limestone lay deposits of haematite which, rich in iron and with a deep red

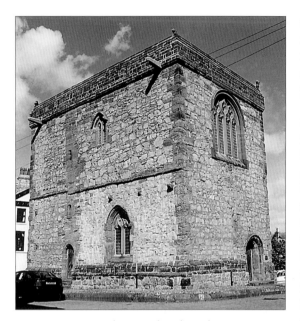

133   Dalton Castle, where the Court Leet was held.

colour, was mixed with a poorer grade ore to yield pig-iron of a type suitable for making cast and wrought iron. The ore also played a significant role in the production of steel.

In the early days, ore taken from shallow pits was conveyed to furnaces for smelting, some of it to South Wales. In general terms, ore recovered from pits on the eastern side of Dalton went in horse-drawn carts to bayside piers, such as those at Greenodd and Conishead Bank; ore from the west of the town, transported to Barrow, was tipped on the shore prior to being loaded on ships. Such congestion of horse-drawn traffic occurred that the idea of constructing a railway was mooted. Local people spoke with awe of the sinking at Park in 1850 of a pit, named Burlington as an acknowledgement of ducal support.

With the money allocated for the effort exhausted, the industrialist H.W. Schneider, a considerate employer, was on the point of giving up when the miners persuaded him to continue the quest for ore for one more week, during which time they would work without pay. The deposit of iron ore they encountered that week was so rich and in such quantity that in 1859 an ironworks was established at Barrow to deal with it.

On 22 September 1892 a level in Lowfield Pit collapsed, leading to the subsidence of land at Lindal Bank. A railway locomotive and its tender disappeared forever into the ground, although the footplate crew escaped. When the railway company refilled the hole, the new stretch of track was reinforced using baulks of timber. So vivid was the incident that trains slowed down when passing the spot and an old lady, it is said, was seen standing on one leg at Lindal Bank. She did not want to apply any more weight than was necessary 'gaa-ing o'er 'ere'. John Kay, who completed 50 years of service to the iron ore industry at Lindal, beginning in 1905, told the author of a time when a dozen mines were operating locally. In Kay's day the ranks of the miners included Welshmen and Cornishmen. Cornishmen were great talkers. One said to a Furness man at the start of a shift, 'Will you work while I hold the candle or shall I hold the candle while you work?' The Cornishmen asserted that, before they arrived in the district, the locals did not know how to talk. 'They "cawed" like a lot of crows.'

Mining ended in this area in the early 1940s, when the Nigel Pit, worked by Messrs Kennedy Brothers at Roanhead, closed down, having operated for some twenty years longer than the other pits. The ground was 'heavily watered' and vast sums of money were spent in pumping water from the levels. When Mr Kay was working on the cost sheets at Lowfield Pit before 1914, ore was selling at 12s. 6d. a ton. It was good ore and the price was high. Yet pumping expenses amounted to 3s. 6d. a ton. Local miners said, 'Water got the better of us.' The pit closures presaged a period of industrial depression, when in Dalton and other Furness towns soup kitchens were operating and housewives endured straitened times. Lowfield Pit is now the site of a farm.

Furness Abbey

Stephen, Count of Boulogne and Morton, and future King of England, donated land at Tulketh near Preston to monks of the Order of Savigny, which had been founded in Normandy. Tulketh was abandoned in 1127, and the monks resettled in the suitably isolated district of Furness. Their new quarters were in Beckansgill, the Vale of Nightshade, 'removed from human habitation' and virtually on an island flanked by Morecambe Bay, the marshes of South Westmorland and the Cumbrian Hills. Their basic needs were met by timber, good building stone and a copious supply of fresh water. Not long after they moved, the Savignac Order was merged with the Cistercian Order. The Abbot of Furness, subject to little outside interference and owner of an extensive estate, assumed a status akin to that of a feudal lord. The rapid spread of the Cistercian Order in England and Wales led to the founding of 85 houses, each dedicated to the Virgin Mary. Furness and Whalley were the only two in Lancashire. The Abbey of St Mary, fashioned from the local New Red Sandstone which is easily worked (and just as easily eroded by wind and weather), grew into an impressive range of buildings arranged around a cloister court. The nave and transepts date from the 12th century; the central tower was built in the 15th century. The dormitory, over 200 feet long, was said to be the largest of any English abbey. The monks, clad in undyed wool, worshipped and meditated while the *conversi grangiarii* (lay brothers) did the work, both here and at outlying farmsteads known as granges, six of which are mentioned in a document of 1190. One grange was sited on Walney. So successful were the

134 *Furness Abbey, founded by the monks of the Order of Savigny in 1127.*

135 *William Wordsworth, who was shocked at the railway's proximity to the abbey.*

136 *Monastic gateway at Hawkshead, which was associated with Furness Abbey.*

Furness monks in managing their estates that, among the Cistercian order, only Fountains Abbey, in Yorkshire, surpassed them in terms of wealth. They eventually claimed most of the Furness peninsula, a matter of 55,000 acres, including 11 granges in Low Furness. Furness also held the title deeds to properties in north-west Yorkshire. Daughter houses (missionary bases) were established at Calder in Cumberland, Swineshead in Lincolnshire, Rushen on the Isle of Man and at Iniscoury and Abindon in Ireland. The abbey's seal featured the Virgin and Child in a circle, she with a crown, the nimbus and a globe, he with only the nimbus. On either side were two escutcheons of the House of Lancaster, supported by bundles of nightshade, and charged with the three lions of England. At the base two monks in full habit supported each shield. The foreground featured two plants of nightshade and, over each monk's head, a sprig of the same. A wyvern in the lower compartment was the device of Thomas, Earl of Lancaster.

In the mid-12th century William de Lancaster reached an agreement with the Abbot of Furness with regard to the partitioning of the well-wooded, if hilly, district of High Furness, haunt of buck and doe, wild boar and sow, plus goshawks, the young of which might be trained for falconry. William took the western part and the abbot was content with the east. Yet, woodland being a source of pleasure as well as profit, de Lancaster retained for himself venison and hawks in the whole area in return for a yearly service of 20s. When the agreement about hunting rights was up for confirmation in 1196, Gilbert fitz Reinfred, who had married William's granddaughter, released them to the monks. The abbot, in compensation, granted him Ulverston and all its belongings for 10s. a year. Furness acquired most of Borrowdale in 1209.

The accounts provide us with pictures of medieval toil: of ploughing, manuring, reaping, sheep-clipping, peat-digging and wood-cutting. The tenants of the abbey had work, security and gifts of bread and beer. Every tenant with a plough had the right to send two people to dine in the monastery once a week from Martinmas to Whitsuntide. Children and labourers could go there for meat and drink. The abbot kept secular court at Dalton and had an imposing hall built at Hawkshead for the administration of the northern part of the estate. A statue of St Mary was placed in a niche on the gateway there to accentuate the Furness Abbey connection.

Monastic control saw changes occur in the landscape, though it was not until the latter part of the 13th century that clearance of the High Furness woods began, to make way for sheep. Thomas West, author of *The Antiquities of Furness* (1774), noted, 'At that time, the abbot of Furness, to increase the number of customary tenants, obtained licence of the king, Edward I, to enclose large tracts in Furness Fells which are still known by the name of parks, as Abbot Park, Stott Park, Oxen Park, etc.' The herdwick, a hardy breed of sheep, took its name from the type of farm on which it was kept. By the 14th century the monks had become successful dealers in wool of high quality which was exported from the fine natural harbour in the lee of Piel Island. Alexander Bankes, Abbot of Furness, caused much distress in 1516 when he razed the small farming hamlet of Sellergarth to create more land for sheep. The hamlet was never rebuilt. There was much quarrelling between abbeys, as when Furness disagreed with St Mary's, Lancaster, about fishing rights in the Lune, and with Fountains Abbey in Yorkshire over land rights in Borrowdale.

In 1316 the border nature of Furness became evident, when a force of Scots, elated after success at Bannockburn, disturbed the monastic calm. Recognising that good quality iron was produced in Furness, they stole all they could find, according to the historian Hollinshead, preferring it to all other plunder. There were two raids, the second and most serious of them, in 1322, being led by Robert the Bruce. The abbot offered accommodation and bribes to the Scots, keen to avoid the violation of abbey lands and dependants. The Scots took the money and enjoyed the hospitality, but then sacked and pillaged land and property, as noted by the *Lanercost Chronicle*: 'Also they went further beyond the sands of Leven to Cartmell and burnt the lands round the Priory of the Black Canons, taking away cattle and spoil. And so they crossed the sands of Kent, as far as the town of Lancaster, which they burnt.'

137 *Detail from the monastic gateway at Hawkshead.*

The halcyon years of Furness Abbey ended with the Dissolution in 1537. Roger Pele, the last abbot, fled, having declined to take part in the northern rebellion that followed talk of Dissolution. He was subsequently given the position of Rector of Dalton. The commissioners who dealt with the material matters concerning Furness Abbey's estates took into account 'moche wood growing in Furneysfells in the mounteynes there as Byrk, Holey, Ashe, Ellers, lying lytell shorte okes and other Undrewood but no timber of any valewe.' It was noted that the abbots of Furness 'have been accustomed to have a Smythey and sometyme two or thre kepte for making of Yron to the use of their Monastery'.

The commissioners also listed the customs, such as pannage, charcoal-burning and *greenhew*, the latter being payment by tenants for the right to cut underwood. The woods were coppiced for *bastyng* (basket-making) and *bleckyng*, the making of potash, an ingredient in soap-making for the textile industry. A dozen, mainly small, woods that belonged to Furness Abbey were still being rigorously managed. Oak trees were valued as timber, the underwood being cut for fuel on rotation. In the 17th and 18th centuries the woods were carefully managed to provide the iron industry with charcoal for smelting.

When Wordsworth visited the area, some navvies working on the new railway line were looking around the ruins, the beauty of which moved these 'simple-hearted men':

> ...They sit, they walk
> Among the Ruins, but no idle talk
> Is heard; to grave demeanour all are bound;
> And from one voice a Hymn with tuneful sound
> Hallows once more the long-deserted Quire
> And thrills the old sepulchral earth around.

In 1864 Mrs E. Lynn Linton shook her head sadly and wrote, 'And now in these glorious grounds, where formerly the mighty Abbot and his monks walked, prayed and framed the laws of their generation, is a grand hotel for summer tourists, full of all modern luxury and modern self-assertion.' The name of *Furness Abbey Hotel* was, she added, an essay in itself on the changing nature of society.

Barrow

The approach to Barrow is along Abbey Road, which is broad, tree-lined and usually breezy. Local people must have been thankful for the sea breezes during the dirtiest phase of industrialisation; the polluted air would have been blown away. The Norse settlers called this place Barrai (Bare Island); it is just one of a cluster of islands lying to the west of Morecambe Bay. Norman Nicholson, the Millom poet, wrote, 'At high tide, the sea is round three sides of Barrow and at all tides the wind blows in clean air from any direction.' In 40 years, which is merely a blink in the story of these bayside villages, Barrow grew from a hamlet to become the world's biggest centre for iron and steel. Dockside cranes looked like thickets of leafless trees, and ships of impressive size were launched, with prayers, into the Walney Channel.

In Barrow's headlong rush for world prominence, encouragement was given by a Bishop of Carlisle who spoke of 'this wonderful town' as 'one of the miracles of our

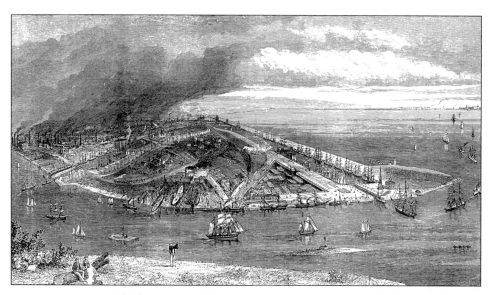

138   *A bird's-eye view of Barrow-in-Furness in its Victorian heyday.*

time'. He found himself looking upon it 'with the same sort of ignorant wonder with which people regard the pyramids'. He questioned how it had been built and what was to become of it if it continued to expand at its present rate. Doreen Wallace observed in 1940 that Barrow had not much to interest the antiquary, 'for it is almost entirely of the Late Industrial period; however, it is late enough to be well planned and its cleanliness shows a high degree of civic pride on the part of the inhabitants'.

In 1836 Barrow was described as 'the principal port of Furness for the exportation of iron ore and also visited for sea bathing'. The place was still much smaller than Dalton, for the port facilities did not need a large labour force. In 1842 it was a mere 150, rising to 325 by 1846 and to 661 in mid-century. The Furness Railway, created with financial backing from influential folk including the Dukes of Devonshire and Buccleuch, opened in 1846 and connected the mines of Lindal and the slate quarries at Kirkby with the unpretentious harbour at Barrow (then just a glorified creek under the Port of Lancaster). The railway company subsequently laid out huge docks, aiming to make Barrow a centre of world trade. By 1864 the local population was over 8,000; this figure doubled in the next two years.

Among the most notable men to be associated with Barrow's startling Victorian rise to industrial prominence were Ramsden and Schneider. Nor should we forget William, 7th Duke of Devonshire (1808-91), whose support of the Furness Railway led the company to display the Cavendish motto, *Cavendo Tutus*. Sir James Ramsden, civic leader, industrialist and social worker, insisted on spacious thoroughfares and the latest ideas in town planning. So the town was built on the pattern of a grid, with the broadest streets flanked by trees. The local people thought so much of Ramsden that they unveiled a statue of him while he was still alive. Young and energetic at the time when booming Barrow needed him, Ramsden presided over the engineering department of the Furness Railway, rose to the rank of general manager and became a director.

139   *The cranes of Barrow shipyard as seen from the Walney Channel.*

Stories of the life and works of Henry William Schneider continue to enthral. He arrived on the Furness scene in 1839. This young merchant, speculator and industrialist found the iron trade appealing and became, in the words of social historians J.D. Marshall and John Walton, 'incomparably the most astute capitalist in Furness'. The Schneiders had settled in England during the 18th century, becoming respected London merchants with a special interest in mining, both at home and abroad. London-born, but from a Swiss family, Henry lived in the city but put down roots in Furness. He married his first wife, Augusta, daughter of a business associate, at Urswick parish church in 1842. She had been reared at a grand house in the village. In 20 years of marriage she bore Henry three sons, but died while still relatively young. His second wife, Elizabeth, daughter of Canon Joseph Turner, Vicar of Lancaster, bore him four daughters. She died when the Schneiders were holidaying on the Continent.

Schneider's nimble mind and zestful manner led to a rapid expansion of the iron ore industry in Furness. In 1851, with Robert Hannay, he began the construction of iron furnaces at Hindpool; they were operating two years later. Schneider's vision, persistence and entrepreneurial flair, in addition to his choice of associates, led to the establishment of iron and steel works at Barrow in 1859. In 1866 the ironworks were amalgamated with a steel company launched by Ramsden. Sixteen furnaces stained the night sky. After spending over £30,000 prospecting for ore in Furness he discovered a large deposit at Park Knotts, near Dalton. This became the most profitable mine in Furness. By 1876 Schneider presided over the world's largest steelworks and, the roads having become clogged with horses and carts, a railway had been built to convey iron ore, slate and limestone to a new deep-water port. A.G. Banks, the biographer of Schneider, described him to the author as 'a generous if somewhat autocratic benefactor'. He also told a story of the time when the use of Piel as the shipping point for the ore trade led to Schneider buying three steamships and operating them between Barrow and other ports, including Fleetwood. But the ships proved so expensive to operate that the engines were removed and the vessels were converted to sail.

Schneider had a London home but eventually became a man of two north country worlds: the stressful business and public life of Barrow and the more languid retreat at Belsfield. This mansion, of Italianate style, stood in its own grounds with a view of Bowness Bay and the fells beyond Windermere. It had been built for the Baroness de Sternberg in the 1840s. Schneider purchased it in 1869 and promptly hired a score of people to form his domestic staff and a similar number to tend the large gardens. He then took on the unelected role of local squire. Bowness saw a good deal of him; he was benevolent in his support of the church and generous to the working classes. He died at Belsfield, in 1887, aged 72 years. A poem that appeared in the *Barrow Herald* contained the lines, 'For now the fraternal link is broken / And rich and poor alike have lost a friend.'

The existence of the 'Esperance' pier in Bowness Bay reminded local people of Schneider's years at Belsfield. He had used the *Esperance* to get to work in Barrow. The sleek craft was distinctive, being an iron-hulled steam yacht made with a hull of high quality iron by T.B. Seath and Company, of Rutherglen. With a length of 75 feet, she was the first twin-screw vessel to be driven by engines of the compound type. On completion on the Clyde, she travelled under her own steam to Barrow, where she was placed on wagons of a special type for the last few miles by rail to Lakeside, sliding gently into Windermere in March 1870. Almost the whole village turned out to see (and admire) this stylish vessel.

On a working day Schneider would stroll through the grounds of Belsfield on his way to the pier. His butler, Mr Pittaway, preceded him, carrying breakfast on a silver tray. Crewed by two men, the *Esperance* cruised the seven miles to Lakeside in less than an hour. Schneider could watch the passage of the wooded shore and the miniature mansions of others who had done well during the industrialisation of England. At Lakeside he would be directed to his special coach on the Barrow train (he was one of the directors of the Furness Railway). A secretary was on hand to deal with business matters.

James Ramsden, superintendent of the railway, dreaming of 'a new Barrow', devised the layout of the town, which impresses a stranger by its neatness. Graceful squares, named after Ramsden and Schneider respectively, lie at the two main intersections. The docks of Barrow, authorised by an Act of 1863, conveniently occupied the area between the mainland and Old Barrow Island. The town was established as a municipal borough in 1867. The Devonshire, first of the big docks, was opened in the same year. At the opening, by the Duke of Devonshire, the guest of honour was Mr Gladstone. *Punch*, the satirical magazine, observed that Barrow had swelled, almost within the memory of the youngest inhabitant, from the quiet coastal nest of some five score fishermen into 'the busy, bustling, money-making, money-spending, roaring, tearing, swearing, steaming, sweltering seat of 20,000 iron-workers'.

In 1881 steamer services that had operated from the pier on Roa island to the Isle of Man and Belfast were transferred to Ramsden Dock at Barrow, where a new station was opened for connecting trains. The service was well patronised until, in 1904, the Midland Railway opened its new harbour at Heysham, but steamer services continued to operate across Morecambe Bay to Fleetwood and Southport until the First World War. *Lady Moyra*, the best known of the Barrow-Fleetwood steamers,

140   *H.W. Schneider, an astute industrialist,*
expanded the iron industry of Furness.

crossed Morecambe Bay for the last time in September 1914, and from 1919 she served in the Bristol Channel. (The gallant ship was sunk at Dunkirk in the Second World War.)

Despite early optimism, Barrow was not to become the main port on the west coast. When the haematite of the 1880s lost its monopoly of the steel trade, the Furness Railway had to realign itself towards tourism. Barrow's population peaked at 74,000 in 1931, since when there has been a steady decline. During a golden age of ship-building, liners and warships were launched into the Walney Channel. James Ramsden had begun a naval construction works but from 1897 the ship-building firm was Vickers. *Dreadnought*, the first British submarine to be atomically propelled, was built here. When the *British Admiral*, a 100,000-ton oil tanker, slid into the Walney Channel, Barrovians held their breath, anxious that it would take a slice from the island. The demand for nuclear submarines led to the construction of an enormous building within which they could take shape.

Barrow has lost its iron furnaces, railway works, jute manufacturing, salt works and other notable industries but has won a share of the present hi-tech age. Natural gas from an offshore field piped ashore at Barrow supplies 10 per cent of Britain's gas demand and is expected to last for 40 years. The so-called Morecambe Field is actually 26 miles west of Blackpool. Gas was first piped ashore here on 8 January 1985, transported through a marine pipeline 25 miles long. Once ashore, it is dried and given a gassy smell (for safety) before being fed into the National Gas Transmission system. Offshore wind energy, produced by between 20 and 30 turbines, is proposed for a site six miles off Walney Island; it will be an impressive spectacle, but not one that will enhance the seascape.

Twelve

ISLANDS OF MORECAMBE BAY

When the weather was becoming more moderate with the melting of glacial ice, humans on Walney Island lived the simple life, using pieces of flint found on the beaches for making tools, and laboriously gathering shellfish to sustain their basic diet. Nesting seabirds would provide them with meat and eggs. At the north end of Walney, evidence of occupation from Neolithic to Viking times has been found. Rough outs from the Langdale stone axe factory, discovered in 1947, indicated that pieces of this volcanic tuff, intended for axe-heads, were roughly blocked *in situ* and finished in Furness settlements and elsewhere before being traded over a wide area.

Walney was the largest of a group of low-lying, sandy islands at the tip of the Furness peninsula which appeared in the last phase of what is popularly known as the Ice Age. Retreating ice left rock, sand and clay at the mercy of wind and wave. Walney, the most southerly point of the county of Cumbria, is tethered to the mainland by a bridge; it became a dormitory to Barrow when the firm of Vickers built a town for its skilled workforce and their families. Roa and Foulney were provided with a causeway. Piel and Sheep Island are tide-washed on all sides but may be reached at low tide by those in the know. The islets of Barrow and Ramsey were long since lost in a dockyard complex.

Walney

About the same size and shape as Windermere, the island of Walney is reputedly the windiest lowland site in Britain, though it does form a natural breakwater for Barrow. The tides have modified its shape over the years, battering and eroding the western shore. On the eastern side erosion has been less dynamic and the coast features mudflats and shallow bays, a delight for birds. It is low-lying, with sand dunes to the north and south. In the central area red boulder clay is evident. Walney lost its island flavour in 1908 when Messrs Vickers replaced a steam ferry from Barrow with an impressive bridge that cost £160,000. A new suburb, Vickerstown, came into being on Walney; it is home to over 11,000 people.

Once the property of Furness Abbey, Walney became a 'walled island' because of the dikes raised to keep the sea at bay. Dike Days were held for their repair, though the tide crossed the island several times in the 18th century. Pastor West, who wrote a guidebook in 1805, commented that an industrious people would long since have joined Walney to the mainland by a sea-bank: it had been battered by the tides, yet

141 *Walter Shepherd, who cared for the South Walney reserve for many years.*

142 *An oystercatcher, one of the common nesting species on South Walney.*

'the inhabitants seem almost insensible of any danger or loss'. Fifty years ago, the flow tide was still threatening to break the island into two.

Talk at Biggar, which lies to the south of Vickerstown, was mainly about farming and fishing in those days. Farmers had difficulty in making a living on land that was either clay or gravel. Biggar was governed by a Grave, who had two assistants. It was the Grave's duty to find lodgings for the herds who, with help from their dogs, cared for cattle on the common from May to October. This custom, which might have begun in monastic times, lasted until 1945, when the last Grave, H.S. Senogles, of Piel View Farm, wrote in the minute book, 'the end of a perfect day'. Old-time Biggar was not conspicuous when viewed from the sea. It also had elements of a fortified settlement: no door or window faced outwards, for a betraying light would attract pirates or privateers. The islanders, noted wreckers, lured vessels to destruction on the beach by simulating a ship's light and thereby indicating safe waters. At the *Queen's Arms* at Biggar, beams of black Spanish oak were said to have come from a wrecked galleon of the Armada.

Vickerstown occupies a prominent central position on the island but the northern and southern ends are dedicated to nature conservation. Miss A.M. Wakefield, visiting Walney in 1909, was shown the 'gull settlement' at the south end. Some years before, the birds had bred at the north end, 'but that proved too near the Barrow mill hands'. When they switched to the south end the Duke of Buccleuch, who owned the island, restricted human visitors to those holding tickets of admission. With such protection, the gulls flourished in greater numbers than ever. Miss Wakefield and her friends sailed from Piel Island to Haws Point on

143 *The nature reserve on South Walney in the 1960s.*

Walney and looked in vain for the old watcher who should have checked their tickets. He preferred the other, more sociable end of the island and 'troubles neither the gulls nor the rare visitors'. She wrote of the nesting birds: 'Rising from their nests, they shriek and scream and fight among themselves, till the whole air for many hundred yards seems like a huge ill-conditioned aviary.' Farming folk slyly took many of the eggs which 'mak' a good coostard, and we loike 'em fried'. A Walney resident remarked with pride that 'many a sack o' them swaller eggs [those laid by terns] have ah give't tu't pigs!'

In 1963, at the invitation of R.E.O. Cavendish of Holker Hall, the south end of Walney Island was established as a nature reserve. The Lancashire Naturalists' Trust and the Lake District Naturalists' Trust collaborated to manage the 130-hectare reserve and appointed a full-time warden. It is now a reserve of the Cumbrian Wildlife Trust, with five miles of nature trails and eight hides overlooking varied habitats. Scheduled as a Site of Special Scientific Interest by the Nature Conservancy as long ago as 1951, its main feature is a mixed nesting colony of about 20,000 pairs of herring and lesser black-backed gulls. Here, too, is the most southerly breeding colony of eider in Britain.

144 Walney has a huge mixed colony of gulls. Pictured at its nest is a herring gull.

145 *An eider duck, sitting firmly on its Walney nest.*

Nesting species include little tern, ringed plover, shelduck and oystercatcher. Birds share the ground with lizard, natterjack toad and palmate newt. Walter Shepherd helped to protect the birds for a quarter of a century. The natterjack toad, the rarest amphibian in Britain, is also found to the north of the island, where a 650-hectare patchwork of sand dunes, dune heath, salt marsh, shingle and inter-tidal mudflats, spangled with over 350 plant species, forms a National Nature Reserve. On the stable shingle grow Ray's knotgrass, Portland spurge and the Isle of Man cabbage.

At the southernmost end of the island, seven miles from Biggar, is a lighthouse, now automatic but not so long ago the home and workplace of a lady lighthouse keeper. When the lighthouse was built on a drift deposit in 1790, it was to direct ships being used in the Jamaica rum trade and heading for Glasson Dock, by the Lune. William, the last of the Geldart family to live at the lighthouse, borrowed a horse and cart from a farm to collect the oil that kept the navigational light burning. Gone from South Walney is the jetty from which boats sailed with cargoes of salt. A market in sand and gravel succeeded this trade, both materials being needed for building work in the burgeoning industrial towns of Lancashire.

146   *One of the Walney sandpits from where material was shipped to the burgeoning towns of Lancashire.*

147   *A lighthouse on South Walney, built in 1790 to guide ships to Glasson Dock on the Lune.*

Piel

Lying half a mile off Roa, the island of Piel is reached by ferryboat. William Wordsworth, who dwelt in sight of Piel for 'four summer months', described its form as 'sleeping on a glassy sea'. To the Scandinavian settlers this was Foudray, or Fotheray, meaning 'fire island', the fire being a beacon designed to guide boats. When Furness Abbey evolved into a commercial as well as a spiritual centre, Piel came into its own, providing not only a harbour but land on which a warehouse might be built to keep cargoes safe from raiders. The first tower was constructed of wood, but was replaced early in the 14th century by one of stone, complete with defensive ditches, to ward off invaders; it would become known as a castle. In the year 1212, when the local harvest failed, the abbey received from King John a licence to permit the monks to land a cargo of 'wheat, flour and other provisions' to stave off famine. An unlimited cargo licence followed in 1232; the abbey's ships came under royal protection in 1258. In 1450, at a time of high trade tariffs, the abbot was in the smuggling business, handling wine and other illicit goods.

Smuggling was a local occupation in 1487 when Lambert Simnel, a merchant's son and pretender to the English throne, landed at Piel from Ireland. He held court in the castle, then resumed his journey to London, with German and Irish mercenaries, to make a bid for the Crown, a bid that ended with defeat in battle at Stoke. Back on Piel local people merely shrugged their shoulders and continued their trading and

148 *A former 'king' of Piel and his wife.*

149 *Piel Castle was built as a warehouse by the Furness monks.*

smuggling. Nearly two centuries later there was an official visit by revenue officers from Lancaster who had heard that smuggling was on the increase. They set about destroying this 'fraudulent trade'.

In 1588 Piel was reported to Elizabeth as being the only good haven for great ships between Milford Haven and Scotland. At the time of the Armada it was named as one of the places for the likely landing of the Spaniards for two reasons: it had a fine harbour, and the deputy lieutenant of Piel was a Catholic.

It was on Piel, according to Gerard, the 16th-century herbalist, that the barnacle goose was bred from barnacles. The legend began when someone noticed that a certain type of barnacle had 'feathers' and 'legs', and the commonest species of local goose became known as a barnacle! John Hudson, a writer of the 1840s, saw Piel when 'it was enlivened by vessels which had run in for safety or to await a wind to waft them into Fleetwood or Liverpool. The masts are sometimes almost countless there.' Hudson boarded a boat from Roe [*sic*] to Piel. He was taken across the stretch of water known as Piel Harbour, 'a beautifully broad and deep channel. Her Majesty's navy could shelter there and, were the ships once in, they would lie as still as in a dock'.

The Duke of Buccleuch gave the island of Piel to the people of Barrow. The castle is now owned by English Heritage. Most people access the island by private craft or ferry based at the tip of Roa, where the channel is violent when stirred by wind, having a 20-foot rise and fall of water. Thomas Swarbrick, an old-time ferryman, had a sailing boat 26 feet long with a beam of almost eight feet. James Moore, a ferryman in recent times, had a boat driven by engine which he used to transport young sheep reared at Ulpha in the Lake District to the island where, the climate being more moderate than in the Lakes, they spent the winter cropping the rich grass. Moore related that, in the days of 'wooden ships and iron men', pilots lived on Piel. An old fisherman's tale relates when up to 20 boats anchored at Sandgate went out with the tide to collect mussels off Piel using 'big, long-shafted drags' to free the shellfish from the rocks. One day, tragedy befell the Robinson family. The fishermen had loaded up the boats with mussels and were returning home on wild, rough water. It was decided to anchor for a while before crossing the most exposed stretch, but the Robinson lads continued. 'They had a lot of mussels in the boat which got to bumping and banging. The boat sank – and the lads were drowned.'

A row of eight cottages, built for coastguards, still stands in Piel. The *Ship Inn* has a royal publican. Since the days of Lambert Simnel, who declared himself King of England, the landlords have been 'kings' of the island. To become a Knight of the Ancient Order of Piel Castle, the landlord or an existing Knight performs a ceremony in which the applicant, occupying a special oaken chair, provides 'drinks all round'. A woman becomes a Baroness. He who becomes a Knight undertakes to be on continual good behaviour, steady, 'and at all times attentive to the opposite sex'. He assists the king if sports are organised. The official sports are 'boat-racing, cock-fighting, bull-baiting or pigeon-shooting'. Any member unfortunate enough to be 'wrecked and drowned' on Piel Island is at liberty to go to the *Ship* and demand a free night's lodging and as much as he might eat or drink. In 1960 Dan Rooney, along with his wife, was the only permanent inhabitant of Piel who held this position.

150 *Roa Island, long attached to the mainland by a causeway.*

151   *A Roa ferryman, providing a waterborne link with Piel Island.*

Roa

If you expect to visit a rocky, sea-girt island with smugglers' caves and laughing gulls, Roa will be a disappointment. It lost its island status in Victorian times when a causeway was made by the Furness Railway Company. The causeway has since been urbanised and is flanked by lamp standards. When there was a railway branch line along the causeway Irish cattle were landed here. The railway was ripped up in the 1940s, the causeway was widened and footpaths created. Schneider, the tycoon, had a stylish residence here.

A conspicuous structure at the tip of Roa is a lifeboat station on stilts. The first lifeboat, known as the *Commercial Traveller*, operated from 1864 until 1878 and rescued 16 people. It was succeeded by the *William Birkett* and, successively, by the *Second William Birkett* and the *Thomas Fielden*; the latter put to sea for the last time in 1901, not having been called upon to perform a single rescue. The *Second Thomas Fielden*, in contrast, rescued 45 people and last saw service in 1927. In September 1958, when the lifeboat stationed at Roa was called *Herbert Leigh*, a sick man was landed from the Morecambe Bay Light Vessel. In a rough sea, the crew had been forced to keep the craft running into the gale, eventually landing the casualty at Moelfre, on Anglesey. A foot of water having formed in the engine room, the lifeboat had to be taken to a boathouse for examination, and the crew, in jerseys, sea boots and oilskins, returned home by train.

Foulney

This diamond-shaped island of sand and shingle overlying boulder clay is connected to the mainland by a causeway and a shingle ridge. Foulney, well covered by vegetation, is said to have been known as Fowle Island, a Scandinavian term alluding to the abundance of nesting seabirds. It would have been an island at that time, though the mainland was still accessible on foot at low tide. Foulney came into the domain of Furness Abbey. A 16th-century document relating to the abbey's revenues mentioned that bird eggs 'were always reserved to the use of the said late monastery for the expenses of the same'. On the island were 'innumerable fowle of dyvers kyndes upon the erth emongs the grasse and stones, for there ys neither tree nor bushe growinge there'. Many writers have waxed enthusiastically about the concentration of nests in spring and early summer. Nests were so near together that 'neither man nor beaste can pass through it without great distruccyon to the eggs'.

Foulney was tethered to the Roa causeway to curb the ebb tide that, on sweeping round by Ulverston, had deposited silt in a channel being used by boats. A fierce tide, over-running parts of Foulney, may carry away a mass of material and heap it up not far away. The island is forever changing its size and shape, but was once reckoned to extend to 28 acres. From the main island runs a spit, known as the Slitch Ridge, that enfolds a shallow bay. Hereabout nest terns, otherwise known as 'sea swallows'. Their flickering forms, backlit against the blue of a springtime sky, appear to be transparent. Disappointingly, for creatures so light and graceful, the voices of the birds grate on the ears.

152   *Common terns on Foulney, which is said to be named after its abundance of birds.*

The flow tide litters Foulney's beaches with rubbish, including heaps of mussel shells. So dense were the mussel beds that parts of the Bay were blackened by them. The area supports a formidable number of eider ducks. Foulney has recently been popular with those collecting shellfish. It has long appealed to anglers, providing excellent fishing for sea bass.

Morecambe Bay, playground of wind, tide and river, is changeable but unspoilt. It is an area of enormous variety, featuring sandbars and skeers, sandflats and mudflats, salt marshes and shingle spits. Doreen Wallace, travelling between Greenodd and Ulverston by train before the Second World War, enjoyed looking up and down the estuaries.

> Estuarine scenery is one of the great charms of this odd little piece of Lancashire ...
> We are now in the estuary made by the rivers Leven and Crake, the one leading out of
> Windermere and the other out of Coniston Water, and we still have before us the pleasure
> of seeing the tremendous, shining sands which are the mouth of the Kent.

People scutter about the sands at low tide, but at the next flow all traces of their presence are swept away. What can appear desolate and dreary under cloud in actuality teems with life: fluke, shrimp, lugworm, ragworm, cockles, mussels, periwinkles and hairy sea-firs all thrive here, in addition to migratory salmon and sea trout, which pass through on spawning runs to the gravel beds at the headwaters of great rivers. Morecambe Bay is gloriously enhanced when the sun sets in a clear sky and the world goes red. To walk along the promenade at Morecambe at the 'edge of dark' is to appreciate the Bay's vastness against a backdrop of the grey-blue outlines of the Lakeland fells.

GLOSSARY

Balk or baulk . . . . Zigzag structure of wickerwork for catching fish.

Bar . . . . The place where a channel might be forded.

Barfet . . . . Barefoot.

Brack . . . . Piece of sandbar undermined and broken away by the tide.

Brid . . . . A bird.

Carter . . . . Original name for a Sands Guide.

Corf . . . . A fisherman's basket.

Craam . . . . Handfork used by cocklers.

Daan . . . . Dawn.

Dawk . . . . Feeding hole left by a flatfish.

Delve . . . . To dig.

Dike . . . . A ditch.

Ea . . . . Water, also the name of a river on the Cartmel peninsula.

Fluke . . . . A flatfish, common in the Bay. Also known as flounder.

Gaa . . . . To go.

Ginners . . . . . . Gills of a fish.

Gullet or Gunnel . . . . A channel.

Haaf-net . . . . . Net draped from balk for catching salmon and sea trout.

Heft . . . . A handle.

Henpennies . . . Miniscule pink bivalves.

Holm . . . . An island.

Jumbo . . . . Wooden contrivance designed to draw cockles from the sand.

Kewin . . . . A periwinkle.

Knotting . . . . . Net-making.

Laaster . . . . Long-handled, three-pronged fork for spiking fish.

Laik . . . . To play.

Lig . . . . To lie down.

Marsh . . . . Sea-washed turf that provides a winter grazing area for hill sheep.

Melgrave . . . . . Soft spot left by tide.

Mell . . . . A mallet.

Melr . . . . A sand dune.

Muck . . . . Unwanted items in a catch, primarily seaweed.

Picking . . . . Removing husk from a
                     boiled shrimp.
Rank . . . . Abundant.
Rive . . . . To tear.
Roost . . . . Tidal rip.
Talligoram . . . . Coal-fired boiler on
                     a shrimping trawler.
Tangle . . . . Seaweed.
Shellings . . . . . . Droppings left
                     by fluke.

Skeer or
Skear . . . . Outcropping rock
                     on the Sands.
Slape . . . . Slippery.
Snaw broth . . . Melting snow.
Starved . . . . Chilled.
Torf . . . . Turf.
Wammelling . . Fishing with a
                     drift-net.
Wheat . . . . Immature cockles.

Bibliography

Abercrombie, E., *Grange and the Cartmel Fells* (1960)

Allen, S.E. (ed.), *Natural History of the district around Grange-over-Sands* (1975)

Banks, A.G., *H.W. Schneider of Barrow and Bowness* (1984)

Champness, John, *A Walk Around Historic Lancaster* (1977)

Cherry, Peter, *On Morecambe Bay* (1986)

Clare, T., *Archaeological Sites of the Lake District* (1981)

Collingwood, W.G., *The Lake Counties* (1902, 1933 and 1938 edns)

Collins, Herbert C., *Lancashire Plain and Seaboard* (1958)

Cumbria Wildlife Trust, *South Walney* (2003)

Cunliffe, Hugh, *The Story of Sunderland Point* (1984)

Dickinson, J.C., *The Land of Cartmel* (1980)

Ffinch, Michael, *Kendal and the Kent Valley* (1983)

Hindle, Brian Paul, *Roads and Trackways of the Lake District* (1984)

Hudson, John, *Sketches of Grange* (editions of 1850 and 2001)

Jones, Sir Clement, *A Tour in Westmorland* (1948)

Lindop, Grevel, *A Literary Guide to the Lake District* (1988)

Lofthouse, Jessica, *The Curious Traveller: Lancaster to Lakeland* (1981)

Marshall, J.D. and Walton, John K., *The Lake Counties* (1981)

McClintock, Marion, *Heysham Village and Churches* (1984)

Mitchell, W.R., 'Cumbrian Days', *Cumbria* magazine, Vols 1-10 (pseudonym John Armthwaite); *Around Morecambe Bay* (1966); *Across Morecambe Bay* (1973); *Wild Cumbria* (1978); with Bob Swallow, *The Walker's Guide to South-East Lakeland* (1997)

Nicholson, Norman, *Cumberland & Westmorland* (1949); *The Lakers* (1955); *Greater Lakeland* (1969)

Pape, T., *The Sands of Morecambe Bay* (1951)

Pearsall, W.H. and Pennington W., *The Lake District* (1973)

Peter, David, *'Cross Kent Sands* (1985)

Ransome, Arthur, *Autobiography* (1976)

Robinson, Cedric and Mitchell, W.R., *Life Around Morecambe Bay* (1986)

Rollinson, William, *Monastic Low Furness*, Barrow Naturalists' Field Club Proceedings (1963)

Sankey, Raymond, *Barrow in Furness, photographs* (1974)

Stocker, David, *Potted Tales* (1988)

Swale, W.E., *Grange-over-Sands: The Story of a Gentle Township* (1969)

Wakefield, A.M., *Cartmel Priory and Sketches of North Lonsdale* (1909)

Wallace, Doreen, *English Lakeland* (1940)

Waugh, Edwin, *Rambling in the Lake Country* (1861)

West, Thomas, *Antiquities of Furness* (1774)

West, Thomas, *Guide to the Lakes* (1784)

Wilson, John, *The Birds of Morecambe Bay* (1974)

Youth Hostels Association, *The Natural History of Arnside and Silverdale* (1979)

Index

THE IRISH SEA

WALNEY ISLE

North End

South End

Bigger

Sheep Isle

Barrow

Funess Abbey

South End Hawes

Peel Castle

Roe I.

Foulney Isle

Ramside

Leece

D ALTON

Kirkby Ireleth

Titup

Lindal

Stainton

Adgarly

Gleaston Castle

Aldingham

Bardsea Hall

Urswick

Corishead Priory

LOW

FURN

Penn

U

North End Haws

South Scale Haws

Dudd

Cavit House

A MAP

of the

LAKES

in

Cumberland, Westmorland

and

Lancashire.

The Roads as directed in the Guide
are marked thus ————
Other Roads thus ....

Leven and
Ulverston Sands

Chapel Isle

Holker Gate
Holker

Cartmel
Wells

Flookboro

Humphry Point

Carter House
Grange

C

Heysham Point

Poulton

Torrisholm

Overton

Hest Bank

Lancaster Sands

IRNSIDE
FELLS
Irnside
Tower

Ashton Hall

Scale
Hall

Slyne

Bolton

Leighton Hall

Furnace

Dallam Tower
Par

Betham

Castle

LANCASTER

Skerton

Lune River

Beacon

Warton

Yealands

OF

Beela

R

Carnforth

Borwick

BURTON

Kellet

To Preston

To Kirby Lonsdale

PART

FARLETON
KNOT

Scale of Miles.

1   2   3   4   5